Senior Management in Schools: a survival guide

Marilyn Nathan

BLACKWELL
Education

© Marilyn Nathan 1991

First published 1991

Published by
Basil Blackwell Ltd
108 Cowley Road
Oxford OX4 1JF
England

British Library Cataloguing in Publication Data
Nathan, Marilyn
Senior management in Schools : a survival guide.
1. Great Britain.   Administration
I. Title
373.1200941

ISBN 0–631–18008–7 (pb)
ISBN 0–631–18092–3 (hb)

Typeset in 11/13 pt Plantin
by Graphicraft Typesetters Ltd, Hong Kong
Printed in Great Britain by T.J. Press (Padstow) Ltd.

Contents

Introduction

What is the purpose of this book?

This book is a practical handbook for senior managers in schools. It explores the main functions of senior management and provides the kind of information, advice and ideas you might find useful if you have, or are about to take on, a senior management post.

We hope that three broad groups of senior managers will find this book helpful:

1 *New senior teachers or Deputy Heads*
A main purpose of this book is to provide guidance for those about to take on a senior management role or those who have recently been promoted to a deputy head position. There is a lot of difference between being a middle or a senior manager in a school. Learning to cope with your new role successfully can be a problem and you are unlikely to find that your LEA will offer you much induction. This book hopes to help you understand and adjust to your new role.

2 *Aspiring senior managers/Deputy Heads*
This book also aims to help would-be senior managers. If you have a clear understanding of what being a senior manager entails, you are much more likely to be convincing at interview than if you can only talk about the work of your present department.

3 *Experienced senior managers*
Are you finding that you have to run in order to stand still? Nowadays a successful senior manager needs a very high level of

management skills and access to up-to-date information about current issues. Thus if you have been in post for some years you may be realising that your job has changed significantly or you may recently have been given new responsibilities in the senior team. The team itself may have changed its membership or expanded. Our aim is thus to help existing senior managers cope successfully with the complex demands of the modern education system.

Who are the senior managers in a school?

In the past there were fewer managers at all levels in education. Recent developments, including the 1988 Education Reform Act, have increased the management responsibilities of all teachers. Not only have the numbers of middle managers increased, but, as Heads and Deputies have attempted to shoulder the new burdens imposed upon them, the range of senior management posts has also expanded.

The most important of the school's senior managers are the Deputy Heads. It is now normal for a school to have at least two deputies and some will have as many as four. Their functions and titles vary. The most usual divisions of activity tend to be Curriculum, Pastoral, Community and Administration, but the post may be linked to a section of the school eg Deputy Head Upper School, or to one of the sites on a split-site school. The school may even have taken the decision not to compartmentalise the post of deputy head.

Senior managers in a school may also be the Heads of large departments (eg Science or Modern languages) or Faculties (such as Creative Arts); they may be the co-ordinators of a substantial pastoral area of the school, eg Head of Upper or Lower School, or of a major area of activity eg Curriculum Co-ordinator or Inset Co-ordinator. They are likely to be receiving a grade D or E allowance and be the school's senior teachers. It is rare for responsibility for a department, however large, to be a senior manager's only responsibility.

Figure 1 shows some typical senior management jobs. It is by no means exhaustive and there is some overlap with middle management roles. The TVEI Co-ordinator may be a senior manager in one school and a middle manager in another. Thus where a

Figure 1 *Who are the senior managers in a school?*

particular task appears in the hierarchy of job descriptions indicates how important the school considers it to be. All of the responsibilities listed in the diagram, with the exception of Head of a large department or faculty, may fall to the lot of one of the deputies – or they may be undertaken by a number of different people. Partly this will reflect the number of deputy heads available and partly the philosophy of the school, but in fact, as the diagram indicates, the number of jobs is becoming so great that it is increasingly difficult for them all to be done by a Deputy Head.

Thus although this book could be considered as a guide for Deputy Heads, it is also relevant to anyone who carries out some senior management functions or who is regarded as a member of the senior management team.

What is the senior management team?

The size, composition and power of the senior management team varies from school to school. Its nucleus is always the Head and the Deputies and in some schools they alone will form the team. In other schools it will include the senior teachers. How this group works will be explored more fully in a later chapter, but it generally meets on a regular basis, usually weekly after school, to discuss issues that arise and to formulate policy.

Why do senior managers need a survival guide?

1   *Your role has expanded and become more complex*
Not very long ago the Deputy Headship of a school tended to be considered a terminal post held as a kind of reward by a very experienced member of staff. Now not only is there likely to be more than one deputy, but the deputies are the only members of staff whose contract time does not include a maximum of 1265 hours and the range of duties to be undertaken by a deputy is, if the diagram above is a valid guide, likely to be very wide. The volume and complexity of school management tasks has significantly expanded in recent years. Some of these tasks can be delegated downwards, but the most difficult and complex of them and certainly those that the school or the head considers to be the most important are likely to land in your lap as Deputy Head or a member of the senior management team. Moreover you cannot expect to be able to sort out one complex problem at a time, you have to be able to deal with several at the same time and to be able to react immediately and constructively to externally imposed additional demands. This is one good reason why you might need a survival guide – it could help you increase your effectiveness.

2   *Little training is provided for senior managers*
Another reason why you might need a survival guide is because of the difficulty in finding appropriate training. When we looked at the question of middle management training we found a very varied pattern of provision with a few patches of excellence and large areas where it was virtually neglected. If anything senior management training is in a worse position. Some LEAs do provide induction as an entitlement for new deputies and supplement it with occasional training on specific issues, but in very few LEAs does that amount to more than a day or two per deputy per year.

In the present climate of 'great educational change' this is simply inadequate, particularly when it is contrasted with the numerous training days currently being provided for headteachers. Updating information for deputies is an urgent training need, as is the specific skills training required for new tasks such as financial management, staff development, appraisal, computerisation etc. Some deputies have taken the initiative themselves and have set up self-help training groups, usually working with an area adviser. Even when this exists, however, because of the nature of the Deputy's role it is often difficult for him/her to be able to go out of school to attend a course or training session and even more difficult for all the Deputies to attend the same session.

Then there is the additional problem that even if Deputy Heads are catered for, what about the rest of the senior management team? It is rarely possible to free them as well as a deputy to attend a training session and they are only likely to be sent instead of a deputy if no-one else can go or they are responsible for that particular initiative, eg computerisation or profiling. There are not even many commercial courses for staff at this level of seniority. The onset of GRIST, followed by LEATGS, made secondment for long courses more difficult to support and as you battle through your Open University course in Management in the small hours of the morning, after you have done your marking, prepared your lessons, drafted your whole school policy statement on 'The multicultural curriculum in the light of the National Curriculum' and attended to the needs of your family, you may find a need for a survival guide!

3 *Few books are directed towards Deputy Heads*
'You will see the matter differently when you are a head'. 'You could see that Fred Smith was not a head from the way he talked at the meeting'. Both of these quotations indicate the perceived gap between Headship and other school senior management positions.

In the past few years the number of books written about educational management has greatly increased, but they are directed towards Heads and although they sometimes include the senior management team in their target audience, they are not being written primarily for those who are not yet heads of a school. There are quite a lot of helpful books on particular issues, but few that address themselves specifically to the needs of the senior manager. We hope that this Survival Guide will help to meet those needs.

How to use this book

As a senior manager you will have to examine many aspects of your role in the school:

- What it means to be a senior manager
- How you get started
- How to manage the daily running of the school
- How to manage change
- How to create a development plan
- How to manage Inset and staff development
- How to manage curriculum development
- How to communicate effectively
- How to promote the school
- How to manage the pastoral system
- How to manage resources
- How to manage finance
- How to manage whole school evaluation

These are just some of the areas that you can expect to have to cover as a senior manager in a school. In this book we explore the role of the senior manager and offer practical advice about how to carry out your responsibilities. The way that we have divided the material into sections reflects the areas where we are most frequently asked for advice, though inevitably there will be some overlap.

There are two ways to use this book. You can read it straight through from beginning to end and, particularly if you are a new Deputy Head, you may find that this helps you gain an overview of what the job is like. Alternatively you can dip into it for advice on the aspect of management that is your specific responsibility or one in which you may feel that you need information or support.

Case studies

Integrated through the book is case study material, which will give you the chance to consider and work on 'typical' school management issues. All the chapters include case studies; they are numbered within each particular chapter. Most of the case studies, but not all, focus upon an imaginary school called Bestwick Park, an urban multi-cultural mixed comprehensive school. You will find echoes of your own situation in Bestwick Park even if your own school is neither urban, nor multi-cultural, nor even comprehensive, as the issues outlined in the case studies have relevance to almost all school management situations. There is no need to use the case studies sequentially in order to benefit from them.

There are three categories of case study:

1 *Exemplars*
These are examples of how things are done, such as sample agenda, an example of a staff news bulletin or a school press release.

2 *For reflection*
These case studies invite you to think about the issue raised and often include some discussion points.

3 *For action*
These case studies set out a situation, provide you with information and invite you to consider what action you would take – for example by putting you in the place of the school's Inset Manager who has to prioritise Inset requests, or the Deputy Head who has to counsel a failing member of staff.

Although we offer plenty of advice and ideas that you could adopt or adapt, do remember that there is no 'blueprint' for management. Using our approach and management strategies, however, could help you to become a more effective manager.

1 Getting started

I really had no idea what the job would be like or how to go about it. I was getting bored with running a department so I applied for a post as Deputy Head. I didn't seriously expect to get the job. It was my first application and I hadn't done any management courses or anything like that, but I interviewed very well and was offered the post. Then my troubles started. Nobody bothered to show me the ropes and the LEA didn't provide any induction. The Head wasn't interested in discussing what my job entailed and my job description was extremely vague. I didn't understand the school's procedures or philosophy and I suspect in that first year I probably made every mistake in the book. I kept talking about my previous school until people told me to shut up about it. I had no concept of what it meant to be a senior manager and found it difficult to take a whole school approach. I wasn't very assertive and found it hard initially to ask staff to do duties or to persevere when I failed to get a positive response, so I ended up doing a lot of the work myself. It was the kind of place where we muddled through rather than adopting clear and coherent polices and as I had to deal with a lot of the organisational detail, I took the blame when things went wrong and this seemed to happen all too often. I really learnt the hard way how important it is to be both efficient and effective. I felt very isolated and I know that I was unpopular with the staff. It took me a long time to come to grips with the situation and still longer to start to do something about it ...

(From a Deputy Heads' management conference)

Being promoted to a senior management post is an exciting opportunity for you. But the jump from middle to senior management can feel much greater than the first step onto the management ladder earlier in your career. This Deputy Head's recollections of what it was like to take up a senior management post illustrates some of the difficulties of making that transition. This chapter is designed to help you make the right start. Although we concentrate particularly on taking up a post in a new school, a lot of what we say is still relevant if you have been promoted within your school.

Ten steps to senior management

1   Create yourself an induction programme

If you spend some time in preparing for your new post it is likely to make the first term in the new job much easier for you. You will probably have some spare time before you start the new job which you could use as a period of preparation and induction. The question is, how should you go about preparing yourself? In general what you are going to need is to gather as much information as possible about your new school, to work out what the duties of the new post are and to improve your own skills if necessary.

2   Gathering information

Collect together all available documents and brochures that the school issues. If you have not been given a set of these at interview, ring the school office and ask for them. Read them carefully as they will serve more than one purpose for you:

- First, they will give you a lot of information about how the school operates. The more you know about the school the more confident you are likely to be when you start the job. Asking questions that could be answered by reading the staff handbook simply makes a bad impression.
- Second, the brochures will give you an indication of the school's working philosophy. You are unlikely to have been appointed to the post if you are totally unsympathetic to this

philosophy, but even if you are in broad agreement, you do need to understand it clearly.

• Third, look at how the brochures are presented. Are they all the work of one writer? Is there a variety of styles? Do they look good? What impression of the school do you get from these documents? You want to do this because one of your responsibilities, either personally or as a member of the senior management team, may be to market the school and you need to consider how to go about this task.

There may also be statements issued by the LEA about its various policies. Ask if you can be sent copies of any that the school has had to respond to within the last year or that might be relevant to your new post. You will need to compare these with the school's policy statements in order to understand how the school is working within the LEA framework. Remember to ask also for the school's responses to these documents.

This kind of information gathering and background reading should be done *before* you start the new post.

3   Visit the school

Visit the school again if this is at all possible. Unless you have a really understanding Head in your present post, you are unlikely to be able to visit more than a couple of times within school hours, so you need to get the most out of your visits. If the new job is situated not too far from the old one you may be able to join some after-school management meetings. Find out if this is possible because it is excellent induction for you.

Try to attend a school production or function if there is one in the period before you take up your post. It is an opportunity to meet people and to be seen; you will get an idea of what the school is like at its best and how it presents its public image.

4   Meet the Head

You obviously want to spend a lot of time with the Head as you are going to be working much more closely with the Head in a senior management post than as a Head of Department. Your discussion session with the Head should give you some indication of his/her current priorities, how s/he views your role and what s/he expects of you. This should give you some food for thought.

5 Meet the senior staff

A session meeting individual members of the senior staff could be very valuable for you. They are going to be the colleagues with whom you work most closely so it is helpful for you to get to know each other a little before the first day of term. Again it could indicate priorities and how they perceive the team.

Try to meet your predecessor – at best, this can give you valuable insights, at worst, it is politic. Even if the Head has totally redefined the role, it is worth spending a little time with the person who is doing the job now – there may, for example, be things that s/he has had to plan, which you will have to implement.

You cannot expect to get to know the whole staff at this stage and will not wish to create favourites. Just remember to smile and say 'Hello' to anyone you meet around the school on one of your visits.

6 Meet the non-teaching staff

Make sure that you meet some of the ancillary staff. The office staff are going to be your main support in your new post. Go and say hello to the Secretary and her/his staff. Make arrangements for a session shortly after you take up the post, in which s/he explains office procedures to you. This is important – you may be in charge of daily administration and communications, so you need to understand procedures and operate them efficiently.

If the school has a bursar or finance officer, go and introduce yourself. You are likely to be responsible for a number of budgets – Inset, TVEI etc and you will need the bursar's goodwill.

Make sure you meet the caretaker. Liaison with the caretaker is likely to be somewhere on the job description of a senior manager, especially if daily administration or responsibility for the building are among your duties. If the school has a matron, it is a good idea to put her on the list of people you should meet before you start the job. Matron is usually a major support to the pastoral system as well as often dealing with some administration eg supporting the year heads by recording absences etc. If you are to be in

Meet the non-teaching staff

charge of the pastoral system Matron is one of your most valuable assets, so start with her goodwill.

Thus you are meeting people in order to build up your own knowledge of the school as an organisation and to begin to build the goodwill that is of vital importance to you as a manager.

7   Get an impression of the building

Ask for a room plan of the school and then wander around until you understand what the room codes mean and the general layout. Try to get an impression of how good the facilities are. You may shortly be having to arrange room changes for a school which has little free space. Being seen to send 30 pupils to a room which will only hold a small group will not be viewed as a promising start. If you are in charge of some major new initiative you may also have to deal with colleagues making bids for improved facilities and you may need to take decisions which could affect the future development of the school within weeks of having taken up your post. A good time to investigate the facilities could be on an after-school visit when there are not many people about.

8 Clarify what your role is to be

One of the things that you will need to discuss with the Head is what your duties actually are. You will probably have been given a job specification before your interview. Some job descriptions, however, are vague and say that the responsibilities will depend on the skills and abilities of the candidate. If this the case you need to get this sorted out as quickly as possible. Either way you will want to clarify what the tasks and responsibilities actually mean in practice and make sure that you find out what the procedure will be on the first day of term and what part you are expected to play.

9 Decide priorities

Your session with the Head will probably mean that you have been given a lot of work to do. Some tasks may be new to you. There is no need to panic. Just remember the two factors that decide the priority rating of a problem or issue:

- *How urgent is it?*
- *How important is it?*

If you used this technique as a middle manager, you should have no problem applying it to the your new tasks. *Urgent* problems are the things that have to be sorted out at once, eg information to staff that has to be available on the first day. Once you have dealt with the urgent but not serious tasks you can prioritise the others. Some tasks are both urgent and important, others are important but not urgent. What is vital is that you should be clear how demanding the tasks actually are, how much time they will take and in what order they should be done.

10 Improve your skills

As a senior manager you will need to develop your technical knowledge in new areas and improve your management skills. Learning on the job is valuable experience but you want to avoid making too many mistakes as this will not inspire your colleagues with confidence in you as a manager. There are a lot of books available now on specific aspects of management and before you start your new post is a good time to do some reading. If there are courses being offered relating to current curriculum developments or specific skills that you might need eg timetabling, this is a good time to take such a course. It will help you and show your Head that you are developing yourself in order to do the new job well.

Some thoughts for the first term

1   Find out if the LEA has an induction programme for new Deputies. If this exists it could be a valuable support for you.
2   Get to grips with the job from day 1 – it is important never to let the work load get on top of you.
3   There is no need to try to change the world in the first half term, just to prove that you can – this only antagonises people. But if the Head has commissioned you to introduce a major development, do get on with it: you need to show that you can do the job.
4   Make your office look attractive and uncluttered, so that staff and pupils like to come to see you.
5   By the end of the first term try to have spent some time with every member of staff individually, even if this has only been five to ten minutes each.

The role of the senior manager

What are the main differences between middle and senior management?

As Head of Geography I had a very clear area of authority, a clearly defined team and a budget that I could spend as I chose. As Deputy Head I am much more important. Everyone thinks that I have a lot of power and in some ways I do, but my precise area of authority is far from clear; nobody reports directly to me and I have no capitation. I only know that 1265 hours do not apply to me. My role is to do whatever the Head tells me.

(New Deputy Head)

The middle manager

As a middle manager you were the head of a section, usually a department or year group or sometimes a staff team set up to carry out a particular task. You had complete responsibility for your subject or task, a team of staff to lead and capitation to spend. This gave you wide powers – you could be as autocratic as you pleased. It was often not clear who your line manager was, but it was very clear who worked to you.

The senior manager

As a senior manager you are a member of a group of staff who work directly to the Headteacher. Your tasks can vary enormously, so can the size of the senior management team. If you are lucky, you maybe given a specific area of responsibility such as Deputy Head Pastoral, where the components of the job are relatively clear and there is a team of middle managers, eg year heads, for you to lead. More likely you will find yourself having to undertake a real ragbag of jobs. You may find, as in the example above, that there are no staff who work directly to you or that from time to time you have to chair various staff task groups and often that you have to lead more than one team of staff at the same time. The diagram of senior management tasks and roles on page 3 will give you some indication of the kind of duties that a Deputy Head might be expected to undertake.

The Secondary Heads' Association carried out a survey of the duties and responsibilities of Deputy Heads who were members of SHA. The responses indicated over 50 areas of responsibility, which varied from the trivial such as first aid, lost property or litter rota, to the global including curriculum development, staff development and discipline. Thus the job description for a senior management post will depend on how a particular school has decided to allocate the possible tasks between the members of the senior management team.

Analysing your job description

Case Study 1.1   *For reflection*
SENIOR MANAGEMENT
JOB DESCRIPTIONS AT BESTWICK PARK
HIGH SCHOOL

This is an extract from the staff handbook at Bestwick Park High School listing the responsibilities of the Deputy Heads and senior teachers.

The Headteacher is accountable for all aspects of education at Bestwick Park High School. Many of these responsibilities are delegated, as indicated below:

Deputy Head Curriculum
1   Responsibility for timetable planning and construction.
2   Leadership of the curriculum committee.
3   Responsibility for monitoring and evaluating the curriculum and for promoting curriculum development.
4   Responsibility for taking a leading role in developing an equal opportunities, multicultural curriculum, suited to the needs of our pupils.
5   Co-ordination of subject faculties.
6   Liaison with Subject Advisers, Advisory Teachers and other area curriculum leaders.
7   Responsibility for producing the school's 'Option Choices' and 'Into the Sixth Form' brochures.
8   Responsibility, together with the other Deputy Heads, for maintaining overall discipline in the school.
9   Monitoring the work of the senior teachers for staff development and TVEI.
10 Responsibility for staff appraisal.
11 Responsibility for Form 7 and other staff returns.
12 Deputising for the Headteacher as required.
13 Membership of senior management team.

Deputy Head Pastoral
1   Responsibility for the pastoral curriculum.
2   The oversight and co-ordination of the work of the Year heads and their Deputies.
3   Liaison with external agencies such as EWOs, Social Services etc.
4   Responsibility for admissions, transfers etc.
5   Responsibility, together with the other Deputy Heads, for maintaining overall discipline in the school, rewards, sanctions etc.
6   Responsibility for developing a school record of achievement / profile.
7   Liaison with primary schools and responsibility for producing the school's brochure for prospective parents.

8 Responsibility for developing community links.
9 Overall responsibility for the PSE programme.
10 Responsibility for special educational needs.
11 Deputising for the Headteacher as required.
12 Membership of the senior management team.

Deputy Head Administration
1 Responsibility for the daily running of the school, including substitution for staff absences and room changes.
2 Responsibility for the organisation of internal and external examinations.
3 Co-ordination of staff duty teams and construction of staff duty rotas.
4 Liaison with the non-teaching staff such as the caretaker, cleaning staff, groundsmen, ancillaries and lunchtime supervisors etc.
5 Responsibility for probationers and students.
6 Responsibility for the organisation of parents' meetings and other major functions, and for co-ordination of school diary.
7 Responsibility, together with the other Deputy Heads, for maintaining overall discipline in the school.
8 Leadership of the school / governors' finance committee.
9 Responsibility for resources and equipment.
10 Responsibility for Health and Safety, fire drills etc.
11 Deputising for the Headteacher as required.
12 Membership of the senior management team.

Senior Teacher Inset Co-ordinator
1 Responsibility for staff development (other than probationers and students).
2 Leadership of the staff development committee.
3 Responsibility for co-ordinating the school's GRIST arrangements.
4 Responsibility for the dissemination of information about Inservice training.
5 Responsibility for producing the weekly staff information bulletin and for the staff library.
6 Membership of the senior management team.

Senior Teacher TVEI Co-ordinator
1 Responsibility for planning the school's TVEI development and for introducing TVEI into the school.
2 Liaison with the area TVEI co-ordinator, curriculum leaders etc.
3 Responsibility for co-ordinating TVEI initiatives within the school.
4 Membership of the senior management team.

Senior Teacher Head of Sixth Form
1 Responsibility for the overall welfare and academic progress of all sixth form pupils.
2 Leadership of the team of sixth form tutors.
3 Responsibility for sixth form careers education.
4 Writing UCCA and Higher Education references.
5 Liaison with relevant outside agencies.
6 Membership of the senior management team.

These senior staff job descriptions indicate the kinds of task which come within the remit of a senior manager in a school. At Bestwick Park it was decided to group the deputies' jobs into specialist areas: curriculum, pastoral and administrative, and the senior teachers were given responsibilities which at that time were seen as of particular importance to the school such as co-ordination of the TVEI initiative. Often, however, the jobs are scattered almost miscellaneously across the job descriptions, either because they represent a historic division of labours where tasks have simply been appended to someone's job description as they have arisen, or because the Head wishes to give all the deputies a fair division of the more challenging and the more arid tasks or to make easier the rotation of functions. At Bestwick Park, the Head, Brenda Gatlin, has decided to build up specialism in curriculum and pastoral care, because she thinks the amount of technical knowledge now needed to run a school is considerable. In other schools the Head will decide that s/he wants to rotate tasks every few years as this will develop the expertise of the whole team, introduce new perceptions and prevent people from getting stale.

At Bestwick Park this was discussed at a management meeting because the deputies were concerned that staying in one specialism might limit their career opportunities. Mrs Gatlin agreed that she would review the situation after two years. She also suggested that she should set up a shadow senior management structure. This could be useful for them because if, for example, one of the Deputies, who was actively seeking a Headship, succeeded in getting his promotion, the loss of his expertise could damage the team. Having teachers available who already knew how to carry out such jobs as timetabling or cover would ease the transition. Creating a shadow structure could also benefit the scale D and E teachers because it provided on-the-job training opportunities for them to learn about senior management by shadowing the deputies. Because Bestwick Park was a large mixed comprehensive school it had three Deputy Heads and three senior teachers. Many schools have fewer senior managers and it would be difficult to divide up the tasks in this way. What tends to happen is that the administrative duties get divided up between the two Deputies, whose job descriptions are thus simply longer.

The Bestwick Park job descriptions categorised the tasks. In some schools this formidable list would appear much longer because jobs would be listed separately. You would have to start by taking all the jobs which included liaison and grouping them together, or grouping those which were connected with curriculum before you could assess just how heavy your work load is likely to be. You will notice that the Bestwick Park job descriptions do not include any of the more trivial tasks which could burden a senior manager – lost property, litter and graffitti do not appear as such – yet they are implicit in some of the duties. You will notice, too, that some of the duties are the *sole responsibility* of the holder, eg leadership of the curriculum committee, while other tasks appear in more than one job description or are *shared* eg maintenance of overall discipline. In many schools one Deputy has sole responsibility for one of the sites eg upper school.

When you receive your job description read it carefully and check it against the example that we have included here. See whether the responsibilities are strategic or miscellaneous or if there seems to be any rationale to the list. Then look at how heavy the work load seems to be; whether all the tasks are likely to happen at the same time as each other or be spaced out. Try to see how your job description compares with those of the other deputies or members of the senior team. We have tried to show you that it is not a matter of how many items there are, because sometimes one item actually covers a whole group of jobs. Finally it is a good idea to discuss with the Head how s/he interprets your role because it is crucial that you have a clear understanding of your powers and authority if you are to carry out your duties effectively.

Your relationship with the Head

The most sensitive area for you as a senior manager, especially if you are a Deputy Head, is your relationship with the Head. The Head will be the person with whom you are expected to work most closely. What form this working relationship takes will vary from individual to individual. How frequently the Head will consult you, how closely s/he monitors your work and the extent of your powers will depend not only on the Head's personal style, but also on his/her other commitments.

> *Deputy Headteachers ... seem to have the least clearly defined job in the school. The work that Deputies did varies enormously both within and between schools, but many were essentially personal assistants to the Headteacher rather than senior staff with clear and significant responsibilities justifying the status and salary ...*
>
> (Torrington and Weightman
> *The Reality of School Management* 1989)

The quotation from Torrington and Weightman's recent survey of management practice in secondary schools highlights the problem that many Deputy Heads face.

As Deputy Head you hold a very senior position in the school. You are the only member of staff to whom 1265 hours do not apply, as you are expected to assist and support the Head at all times and in any way required. Are you given a strategic area of the school to control and full authority to do so? If you have to deputise during the Head's absence and a crisis arises, will s/he live with the majority of the immediate decisions you have had to take? If so, then Deputy Headship is an exciting, challenging and very rewarding job. If, however, it means serving as dogsbody to a Head who will allow you very little scope to use your own initiative, then Deputyship is a frustrating experience, and it will be difficult for you to justify to other staff your senior status and higher salary. This matters, because the nature of senior management work is not generally understood by the staff as a whole (however much you try to raise awareness) whereas they will be extremely conscious of your lightened timetable.

It is particularly important to establish trust and a good working relationship with the Head right from the start. You need to make the relationship work so that you become a real senior manager, not just a personal assistant to the Head. Remember: most Heads are eminently reasonable people who have been Deputies themselves and who will want their Deputies to succeed; also, managing upwards as well as downwards is a useful skill for Deputies to master.

Case Study 1.2   *For action*
MANAGING THE HEAD

I see one of the main problems for Deputies as their real lack of power. It is not only that they hold most of their authority as part of a team and have to share responsibilities, which does create difficulties, but the real issue is that when they deputise for the Head, because s/he is out of school, when the Head returns, as likely as not any decisions that the Deputy may have made will be rescinded publicly. An example occurred only this week. The Head was out for a couple of days. On the second day a problem arose. I sorted it out and announced the arrangements to the staff. The Head returned the following morning. Her first reaction, publicly in the staffroom, was 'You cannot possibly do that! It will have to be changed.' Whatever her reasons the impression one gets is that she is simply reasserting her authority as Head and of course this undermines my position. I find that I refer problems that as a senior teacher in my last school I would have dealt with automatically, but if I dealt with them here there would be trouble with the Head ...

What advice would you give this Deputy Head?

Some hints for head management

1 Make sure you meet deadlines. The Head needs to be sure that you are efficient.
2 Similarly, work out the details of your super new scheme carefully so that the Head can't just pick holes in it.
3 Always report back – let the Head know that a crisis has occurred and what action you have taken.
4 Never seem to be trying to upstage the Head.
5 Do not give the impression of trying to avoid the more impossible or irritating duties. Show that you can do them and that you are prepared to pull your weight before you attempt to renegotiate your job description.
6 Have your disagreements with the Head in private. Always support the Head in public.

2 The role of the senior management team

You will have noticed that each job description in Case Study 1.1 included 'Membership of the senior management team'. We have said that as a senior manager you are a member of a small group of staff who work directly to the Head and usually very closely with each other. The job of this group is to manage the school. They are the executive team. The overall responsibility of course belongs to the Head, but increasingly the sheer number of tasks makes it necessary for the Head to delegate some tasks to senior members of staff, especially the Deputy Heads.

> *It is becoming increasingly impractical for any one person to encompass the diversity and work necessary to manage and organise a secondary school.*
>
> (Torrington and Weightman
> *The Reality of School Management*, 1989)

Heads are out of school far more than in the past and when they are in school they have to spend much of their time dealing with external relations. This means that the Deputies have the task of managing the day-to-day running of the school. Some larger schools now have as many as four Deputy Heads and two or three Senior Teachers to do this job. As well as seeing that things run smoothly, the senior management team is available as a policy making or advisory group for the Head if s/he so wishes to use it.

When you move up from being a middle manager and join the senior management team, the first thing you must realise is that you are not the leader of the team as you were when you were

Head of Section, but only a member of the team. This is a distinct role change. You may find yourself as the one new member of a well-established team, which expects you to conform to its pattern of working. You may, however, be joining a newly-formed team, eg in a new or reorganised school or one where there have been sufficient changes recently for it to constitute a new team. The team then has to form a group entity and learn to work together. As we saw, most senior managers are given responsibility for a number of tasks and have a mixture of jobs that they do individually and jobs that they do together. Coping with this balance may need some adjustment and working with someone who has been in post a long time and is set in his/her ways may need more than a little tact, especially if you are bursting to experiment with new systems and ideas. Undertaking corporate tasks such as 'Responsibility for maintaining overall discipline in the school' can be difficult; much depends on the personality of the other deputies and how far they are prepared to share power.

As a senior manager you will be expected to take an overview or whole school view, rather than just support the needs of the section for which you happen to be responsible. This can also be a difficult adjustment to make. If the other members of the team have to remind you that you are not the Head of Science any more, you will realise that you are not yet thinking in whole school terms, but are still trying to get the best rooms, equipment etc for your erstwhile department!

Some of the tasks delegated to you are ongoing or are a part of the traditional running of the school eg responsibility for daily cover for absence or for external examinations. You may want to overhaul the system in order to make it more efficient, but the task itself is not new to the school. Increasingly, however, whenever a new task appears – inset arrangements, TVEI, Appraisal, Profiling, etc – the Head will delegate overall responsibility for it to one of the deputies or senior teachers. You will thus find yourself managing the introduction of major changes into the school. This is the area where the Deputy Head's role has changed most over the past few years, to become much more demanding. The sheer number of jobs needing to be done has increased dramatically and it is difficult to find sufficient time to deal with them all especially if the team is small. 82% of the deputies who responded to the SHA survey of Deputy Heads, *If it Moves* ... (1989) had recently assumed extra responsibilities. These centred on introducing, supporting and evaluating curriculum innovation and government initiatives. They involved the drafting of development plans, the enthusing and development of initiative-weary teachers and the maintenance of staff confidence and morale. The creativity as well as the management skills of the senior manager have been seriously put to the test.

Being a member of the senior management team can be a frustrating or rewarding experience depending on how it is managed and what demands it makes. How the team functions will depend on the Head's view of its role; how well it works as team will reflect the Head's ability as a team manager. At its best the senior management team is central to the management of the school, interacting to co-ordinate its smooth running, offering leadership to the many current initiatives and providing a very useful sounding board and executive planning group. At its worst the senior management team is a group of senior staff who neither function as a team nor have a clear role in the school.

A senior manager:
- is part of the executive team
- is expected to be able to take a whole school view
- is expected to contribute to policy making
- has to undertake a lot of responsibilities, which may rotate
- works in association with other team members but reports directly to the Head.

Case Study 2.1   *For reflection*
THE SENIOR MANAGEMENT TEAM AT HILLCLIFFE SCHOOL

Deputy Head 1   Stella occupied a comfortable office next door to the Head's study, and very rarely left it. Her responsibility was for the daily running of the school and for constructing the timetable. Because she dealt with daily cover for absence, she never took or attended school assembly. She was methodical and efficient, but her tasks, although routine, seemed to take up her entire time, and she could be found in her office sorting out cover or calculating the month's total of petty cash from 7.30 in the morning until nearly 5 o'clock at night. Her personal discipline was good, but she took no active part in the pastoral system. Most of the staff were uncertain what her teaching subject really was. She taught Careers and Health Education in the PSE 'circus', but as likely as not, she was too busy to teach her lesson and sent a supply teacher to substitute for her. Nobody could remember when Stella had last been on a course. She said that there were a lot of courses that she would like to attend if only she had the time. The timetable worked in practice, but attracted a lot of criticism from staff, who claimed that Stella always took the easy way out and that timetable decisions were not made on educational grounds. She gave the impression of being preoccupied with the mechanics of the timetable, but otherwise uninterested in curricular matters. Staff went to see Stella if they needed to take time off and required cover; pupils went to see Stella if they wanted to borrow small sums of money – she was known to be a soft touch. Attempting to talk to Stella about a current school initiative or the implications of the most recent Education Act could be embarrassing, yet she had been promoted early, had held her post for several years and was still only 44.

Deputy Head 2   Alan had been appointed Deputy Head Pastoral in the last year of the previous Head's tenure. Everyone had been very pleased to see new blood in the team and there had been a honeymoon period. Alan had seemed affable and to have plenty of ideas. A Pastoral Committee was set up under his leadership and was widely attended. People valued the opportunity to discuss common problems and hoped that this would lead to a much-needed reform of the pastoral system. The committee met regularly but soon criticism was being heard – 'This is just a talking shop; what we need is a structured system with clearly defined procedures which are uniformly enforced ...' No system however emerged and the school muddled on as before. Alan did seem to have an excellent rapport with many of the school's more disaffected pupils and could often be seen laughing and talking on corridors with them, but staff quickly came to realise that if a crisis arose, Alan was not their best bet. Most matters were dealt with, as before, by the hard-pressed Year Heads; if you wanted a pupil interrogated you took him to Don, the Third Deputy, whose reputation alone could cause a pupil to confess without knowing the nature of the charge. If it was a sensitive issue, you went straight to Margaret, the Head. Nevertheless Alan always seemed to be dealing with some pastoral crisis that meant that he was not able to teach his lessons that morning, but Stella was very good at finding a supply to substitute for him. Part of his task was to introduce PSE into the school. Difficulties were anticipated as the previous Head had consulted the staff very little over the matter and many staff were not committed, most lacked confidence, and several were extremely reluctant to participate. Even the most committed staff found Alan's lack of organisation and preparation a serious problem. You often did not know what you were supposed to be teaching that morning until after the lesson had actually started. Discontent with PSE, and with Alan, was reaching considerable proportions.

Deputy Head 3   Don carried out the tasks required of him unquestioningly, but then the tasks were neither numerous nor taxing. He had long been accustomed to hearing himself referred to by the previous Head as 'My strong right arm'. Don enforced discipline and liaised with the police and the caretaker. Mr Frear, the previous Head, had thought it was very important that the school was graffitti free and every Monday morning Don and the caretaker toured the building checking for damage or graffitti. If they found any, Don then arranged to have it cleaned or repaired and interrogated possible suspects. Don also handled one of the school's financial accounts as there was at the time no bursar in post. For this valuable work and so that he should be available in case of trouble Don was given a greatly reduced timetable. Some staff were very critical of Don's role, especially some of the female staff who claimed that by dealing with the symptoms not the causes of the bad behaviour, Don not only failed to solve the problem but in fact made the position more difficult for others as his tough methods made their discipline seem weak by comparison. Many staff felt that Don simply sat in his office for much of the day and considered him an expensive luxury for the school to have to carry.

Margaret, the new Head, found that she had to work very hard indeed to make up for the deficiencies of her senior management team. She managed the curriculum personally, dealing directly with the Heads of Department, and organised the school's programme of staff development. Although technically she had two pastoral co-ordinators of deputy head status, all the more sensitive pastoral problems were referred directly to her. Her team were largely ignored or regarded as useless by the staff; in reality everyone worked round the deputies nor through then, though lip-service was paid to the importance of their role.

The senior management team at Hillcliffe School encapsulates many of the criticisms levelled at Deputy Heads:

1 *Too much time was being spent on routine administration*
Stella was clearly spending most of her time doing routine mechanical administrative tasks. Similarly Don was spending much of his time organising the cleaning of graffitti. Charles Handy was only the first of the writers on educational management to question the benefits or the wisdom of a Deputy Head carrying out trivial clerical tasks which did not involve management skills and which could be delegated to ancillary staff. The recent SHA survey of Deputy Head responsibilities indicated that many deputies still have to spend much of their time on this kind of work. Organising the movement of furniture – eg chairs into or out of the hall – is a typical example. Some administrative jobs however do need considerable interpersonal skills as they involve negotiation and depend for their smooth running upon goodwill. An obvious example of this is cover, which can be an extremely sensitive area to manage. Administration is only likely to be the deputy's main responsibility where there are three or more deputies, because few schools can afford to allow a senior member of staff to spend so much time on it. Providing good administration is an important part of running the school. Creating and establishing appropriate routines and procedures is part of the school's management task, but once they are in place, administration should not occupy more than a small part of a manager's time eg organising school photographs should not take you long after you have done it once or twice. As a senior manager your task is therefore to develop procedures that can be operated in the most time-effective way either by you or by someone else.

2   *They were not using time effectively*

Stella seemed to have a time management problem, because although she had operated the same system for several years she was not on top of it. This gave a poor impression of her capabilities to other staff, as well as making it difficult for Margaret to expand Stella's role. How could Stella be expected to take on the new responsibilities that were evolving after the introduction of LMS if she was already working such long hours? Yet although she was clearly doing more than Don who just sat in his office waiting for a crisis to emerge, her real output was low. It might be more useful for Margaret to explore with her Deputy why routine tasks take Stella so long, than to continue to do so much of the real work herself. Persuading Stella to make the time to go on a Time Management course might help her put things in perspective.

3   *They did not carry out their teaching commitment*

The low teaching load of Deputies in comparison to other teachers can be justified if their management function is visible. Where, like Don, they seem to be doing very little during their non-contact time their light timetable becomes resented by other staff. Where, like Stella and Alan, they do not even carry out their timetable commitments, but constantly send a supply teacher to take their lessons, their credibility wears very thin indeed. Everyone understands a real emergency, but daily emergencies suggest bad management and strain the goodwill of colleagues to the limit. If there is a continuing difficulty then proper timetable provision should be made. A rota of who is free to deal with the crisis should be available. It is inexcusable for senior staff who only teach half a timetable to fix appointments regularly with parents, advisers etc at times when they know they should be teaching.

4   *They were not leading professionals*

It is important to the credibility of a senior manager that the staff believe that he/she was and still is a highly competent teacher. It was difficult for the staff even to guess what Stella's teaching subject had been. That undermined her credibility both as a teacher and as a manager. Heads and Deputies have a role as leading professionals, which Stella clearly cannot carry out convincingly. Indeed, none of the three Deputy Heads had an impressive record as leading exponents of their craft. Moreover neither Stella nor Don were involved in any curriculum development. Stella was the school's timetabler, but she did not lead the curriculum committee and was not on any working parties. Don had occasionally been drafted onto working parties by the previous Head, but that had merely reinforced the staff's suspicion that he had little to offer. Heads of Department went directly to the Head to discuss curriculum matters. In an age of educational innovation it is important that the senior managers are at least aware of what is going on. Even if they do not lead the innovations themselves, they are often called upon to support them and to work with curriculum teams. A significant part of their role is to enthuse and inspire.

5   *They failed to manage*

Both Stella and Don dealt with the tasks that they were given adequately, but Stella was not on top of her job and Don had little to do. Both Deputies were reactive rather than proactive, neither was taking any part in the developments that were taking place in the school and this meant that they were not really acting as managers at all.

Alan seems to have lacked several essential management skills and this caused him to lose the confidence of the staff he was appointed to lead. He was appointed as Pastoral Co-ordinator with the brief to reform the pastoral system and introduce PSE to the curriculum. Staff, however, felt let down because Alan raised hopes of an improved pastoral system and then failed to deliver it. The unproductive meetings provoked resentment because staff had stayed voluntarily after school to attend them. Whatever their feeling about PSE, the teachers had the right to expect either to be involved in the selection of materials for the course or to receive them in sufficient time to think about how they would approach teaching sensitive topics. Alan's ineffective management of the scheme meant that the teachers involved in it did not know what was expected of them. This lost him the support even of the minority of staff who were keen to implement PSE and confirmed the majority in their hostility to the innovation. They came to have a low opinion of him as a manager because of his poor performance and, if he was to regain the respect of the staff, urgent attention needed to be given to how he organised any activity for which he was given responsibility. Indeed the whole team needed to improve their performance as managers.

6   *They failed to give leadership to the staff*
Neither Stella nor Don held responsibility for a strategic management area. Therefore two of the three Deputy Heads did not have leadership roles, which reduced any imput they might make to a management team. They managed tasks but hardly interacted with other staff. They were remote and isolated from the staff, who did not respect them. They seemed to lack the essential interpersonal skills required to carry out a senior management job successfully. What was worse, they did not seem to understand that they needed to have them. Alan did attempt to give leadership, but his poor organisational ability made him ill-equipped to introduce a major change. His failure to organise the preparation of materials for the new PSE programme, provide any Inset for the staff, or to support the initiative through its first year of operation highlighted his inadequacy as a manager. He failed to give leadership when it was needed and he too did not really relate to staff and was not sensitive to their needs. If the team were to perform their function as leaders and managers, Stella and Don needed to be integrated into the initiatives that were taking place, Alan needed to review how he prepared and introduced an initiative and they all needed to work to improve their interpersonal skills.

7   *The Head did the work of the Deputies for them*
Margaret's decision not to try to change the functions of her Deputies but to compensate for their inadequacies by doing more work herself is understandable. She thought poorly of Stella and Don's abilities and worked round rather than through them. She had hoped for more from Alan who had seemed much more in touch, but had been extremely disappointed with his performance and was reluctant to give him another major development to manage. Avoiding using the senior management team and in effect doing their job for them only made their position worse. It confirmed staff, who were already very critical, in their view that the Deputies were useless and it undermined their position. It could not work as a permanent solution, especially as the Deputies were nowhere near retirement age. As LMS got going in the school, Margaret was likely to be out of school much more and would not be able to manage the school's development entirely on her own. To delegate strategic tasks to staff below the Deputies in the hierarchy while they continued to have

an easy time would only focus resentment on an already weak senior management team – so what was she to do?

The team clearly needed a total shakeup. It would be better for Margaret to face with her Deputies the issue of how they were perceived by the staff than to let the situation continue. If that was too difficult, she could approach it by concentrating on the changes to the management structure necessitated by LMS which could provide her with the excuse she needed for major surgery. Her management development plan for the school over the next three years would need to include a complete restructuring of the management team's responsibilities.

A possible scenario could be to put *Don* in charge of the daily running of the school instead of Stella. It would give him more to do, but still would not form a complete task. In addition he could take responsibility for resource management. Training in computerised administration would make it possible for Don to organise the computerisation of the school's record system and to use the Sims system for options and the timetable. This would make him responsible for the work of the school office and he would also need to liaise with the Curriculum Deputy. Giving Don a proper job and increasing his teaching commitment might rehabilitate him in the eyes of the staff.

Stella might benefit from a period of secondment, partly as she needs intensive awareness raising and partly because it would then be easier for her to be moved to different responsibilities. There could be a case for making Stella the school's Pastoral Co-ordinator. She had the administrative skills to create a pastoral structure, had originally gained promotion through the pastoral ladder and was presently teaching careers and health education, though her approach needed updating. Her submerged interest in pupils might revive if she had to take charge of the introduction of profiling and it was possible that as Pastoral Co-ordinator she would be less out of her depth than in leading the school's curriculum development. A good pastoral/PSE course and some strong direction from Margaret about how to manage the initiative could rehabilitate Stella and give her confidence in her own ability. Working with a staff team to develop a structure could help Stella manage time more effectively, particularly if Margaret set them a deadline. Margaret would clearly have to give Stella a lot of guidance, but this was better than having to do all the work herself.

Alan, superficially the best of the team, presents the greatest problem. He needs to be moved out of an area where he has failed, yet this highlights the failure, though an excuse is provided by the complete restructuring of the team. He needs to be given a second chance but in another area. His reputation will go before him and he will need to prove that he is a competent and sensitive manager and leader of staff. The role of Curriculum Co-ordinator would be a real test for him. Support for his organisational/ administrative weakness could be provided by getting Don to check through all Alan's arrangements before they are implemented. Margaret would need to monitor his work particularly carefully – as he is so insensitive to the needs of staff – and to back this with some training for him. Supporting him through the appointment of a Senior Teacher with responsibility for staff development is another possibility. She might also find it beneficial to do some team building work perhaps through a residential weekend involving outside consultants or her Link Adviser. Recent research findings have indicated that in some schools the Deputy Heads do not have a real role and this had led to suggestions that perhaps they are not needed. At a time when great changes are taking place in education and in the way schools are run, and when Heads can be out of school for up to two days per week, there is clearly a job for deputies to do, but they have to show that they can provide leadership and that they are effective managers. It is this challenge that school's senior management teams now face and it could mean that traditional functions are no longer appropriate and that areas of responsibility, as at Highcliffe school, need to be rethought.

Case Study 2.2   *For action*
WORKING WITHIN THE TEAM

How would you cope with these problems?

1 *What I find most difficult is that the Head does not treat us like a team at all. He works with us each as individuals but does not tell the rest of the team what has been arranged – so we never know what is going on and do not function as a team. The result*

is that there is no uniformity of approach. What makes it worse, he cannot see the point in management meetings, which he claims always end up talking about trivia, so we never meet as a group. I have begun to wonder if he actually felt threatened or feared we might gang up against him. It is not what I expected when I was promoted ...

(New Deputy)

2 *When the new Head arrived I was excited. It was like a new start. I waited to be told how he saw my role as I was Director of Studies. But months passed and he did not even seem to want to see me, so in the end I requested an interview. He seemed surprised I wanted to see him. I talked about some of the ideas I had for new courses, and offered to do some of the jobs that I knew that he did not think were going well, but he told me that he was not sure that the time was ripe for curriculum development at the moment and that he would think about my other suggestions, but he never did anything about them. A few months later our Deputy retired and he brought in the Deputy Head from his previous school, who ran the school for him. She knew he did not like to be troubled with things ...*

(Senior teacher)

3 *The worst thing about the senior management meetings is that we seem to talk for ages without actually getting anywhere. The meetings are long without being productive. I think it may help him to talk through things with us but it is very frustrating for us and I notice Susan and Roger keep looking at the clock as the meeting drags on. They are both senior teachers and are attending on a voluntary basis, but we shall lose their goodwill soon ...*

(Deputy Head)

4 *I knew it would be difficult because Jean had been the Deputy for so many years and then we got the additional deputyship and I was promoted. It is very difficult working with her. She has never really accepted me, and does not think that there was any need for another deputy. She interferes all the time, changing or belittling arrangements that I have made, and contradicts me in staff meetings and expects all the interesting or challenging jobs to be allotted to her ...*

(Deputy Head)

5   *The problem is that Alan has never adapted to the demands of the role of a modern deputy. He had been Deputy Head for 19 years and did not see why he should change and anyway I do not think he could. The trouble is that because he is so useless, every time there is something new to do the Head adds it to my responsibilities and it is becoming too much for me to cope with ...*

(Deputy Head)

6   *The trouble with Tom is that he keeps on telling us how much better it was in his last school. We came to dread the phrase. 'At St. Benedicts ...' If it was really so good why didn't he stay there?*

(Staffroom verdict on a new Senior Teacher)

What advice would you give each of these senior managers?

3 Managing for change

Change is an essential function of the managerial role. It may be initiated from within the school or imposed from without. It may take the form of making improvements in the way in which we improve ongoing goals, or we may have to cope with new goals and challenges. In the last twenty years schools have had to carry through a number of radical reorganisations caused by changes in politics, philosophies and birthrates. In the years that lie ahead, the one thing that seems certain is that the rate of technological and social change will, if anything, accelerate and the ability of our pupils to succeed – or indeed survive in a changing environment – will depend upon our ability to adapt the context, methods and ethos of education to the new needs.

(KB Everard and G Morris *Effective School Management*)

Everard and Morris have diagnosed the situation extremely accurately. If you are a senior manager in a school today, you have to manage for change. What does this mean?

First, you have to give leadership to the school during what has been described as 'a period of great educational change'. Over the last few years initiative has succeeded initiative in a seemingly endless stream: GCSE, TVEI, JSA, ERA, LFM, LMS, profiling, appraisal, the National Curriculum. A vast number of changes have been introduced over a very short period of time. Moreover schools have no choice about most of these initiatives; neither about whether to implement them nor the timescale involved. Indeed, it has not just been a matter of one initiative after another, but often of several at the same time.

Second, we have been managing educational change in the context of a society which has been transforming itself at a very fast rate. It has become the task of the educational system not only to equip pupils to become informed, responsible and caring adults, but also to enable them to cope with the demands of a technologically based, enterprise culture. Thus we have had to examine and reform the content of the curriculum, which has itself become more technologically based, and core skills have become an integral part of that curriculum. Learning and teaching strategies have had to become more varied and pupils are being encouraged to take more responsibility for their own learning.

Like it or not, therefore, you have become a manager of development. But what kind of manager do you have to be to cope with this situation? A manager for change will have three outstanding characteristics: S/he will be:

1 *Proactive*
   - S/he will be prepared to use his/her initiative
   - S/he will want to influence change and expect to be able to
2 *Flexible*
   - S/he will be able to adapt to the demands of any situation
3 *Creative*
   - S/he will have vision
   - S/he will see shapes and connections and be able to take a holistic view
   - S/he will have plenty of ideas of his/her own and the ability to build on other people's ideas

Everard and Morris identified the attributes of *positive* and *negative* managers. The positive manager will be able to cope well with management for change and will enjoy the challenge. The negative manager will bemoan the difficulties of his/her situation.

The positive manager
Acts
Accepts responsibility
Is objective
Listens and responds
Proposes solutions
Delegates
Sees opportunities

Has breadth of vision
Faces up to problems
Confronts the source of the problem
Learns
Has foresight

The negative manager
Is a victim
Blames others
Is subjective
Rejects suggestions
Criticises
Is incapable of delegation
Sees threats
Is preoccupied with detail
Conceals problems
Talks about the source of the problem
Is taught
Has hindsight

(From KB Everard and G Morris
Effective School Management)

What kinds of changes are you likely to have to manage?

Figure 2 indicates the range of changes that you are likely to have to introduce. Most change in schools today involves *development*. Curriculum development necessitates staff development; the two aspects are interrelated. You will also be handling organisational and technological development.

A major part of your role as senior manager will be to lead, support and evaluate development. This is the crux of managing for change and this is why managing development is one of the central themes of this book. The chapters on Managing the Pastoral System, Managing Curriculum Development and Introducing Appraisal deal in a variety of ways with handling the complex changes involved in managing development.

If you are going to be responsible for planning and implementing numerous changes in the way that the school is run,

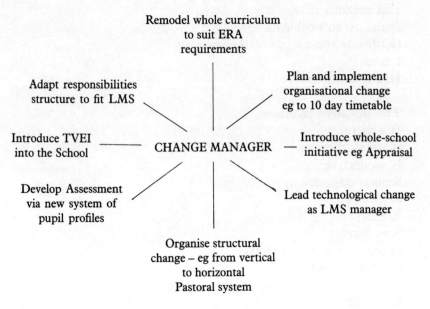

Figure 2

what it teaches, and how, it is important that you do this well –
so how do you manage change?

Case Study 3.1 looks at what can go wrong when an ineffective
manager attempts to change the structure of the school day.

Case Study 3.1   *For reflection*
HOW NOT TO DO IT ...

Brian Harris looked at the staff sprawled in the easy chairs in the
staffroom as he paused before making his next pronouncement. It
was the staff meeting on the first day of the summer term. The
atmosphere was already fraught. There had been several clashes
over items on the agenda and the main item, which he had put at
number five, was still to come. 'Why are they always so difficult?'
he thought to himself, 'Why can't they cooperate? Oh well, I had
better get on with it.'

Brian started to tell them about his great new idea for changing the structure of the school day to remove the lunch hour altogether. He was a lay preacher in his spare time and never lacked for words. The problem was more often to pick out any real information from what he had said. At first the room was quieter than usual. It was rare that he spoke for so long at a meeting without some interruption. 'They are no respecter of persons at Downfell High School,' Brian used to tell his friends at the boatclub, rather ruefully. After all it was better to make a joke of what you couldn't do anything about. Now the silence was total, and he began to feel threatened by it, so he stopped speaking and invited comments.

'What's the point of it?'
'How's it supposed to work, anyway?'
'When are we supposed to have lunch – while we teach?'
'If we do away with the lunch hour we can't run any Games activities and the children won't stay after school.'
'Just because you can't cope with discipline problems at lunchtime, why should we all have to lose our lunch hour?'
'If there isn't a lunch hour we can't talk to each other – are you planning to timetable department meetings during lesson time?'
'It can't be done in the time!'

There didn't seem to be any favourable responses. In the end, Brian brought the meeting to close with the issue unresolved. He was in rather a hurry as he had hoped to spend a couple of hours tinkering with his boat down at the river if he got through the meeting fast enough. 'I expect they will come round in time,' he thought as he cleared his desk rapidly and left. In spite of many reverses, Brian remained the eternal optimist.

They didn't come round, however. In fact opposition to the scheme grew and became extremely vocal: 'The problem is that we don't really see the point of changing the day round at all. Is it just a whim of Brian's or does he really see it as a way of coping with the control problem at lunch time? If he does, he's got it wrong.'
'It seems pointless, and we don't see how it will work.'
'He's such a rotten organiser, if he's really thinking of putting the children into lunch in two shifts, he must have forgotten that

Drama teaches all its lessons in the Hall – where will it go? It uses the Hall because there is no other suitable room.'
'The senior staff looked just as flabbergasted as we did, I bet he hadn't consulted them either. Now they are trying to put the best face on it that they can.'

These comments sum up staff feelings about Brian and the scheme. One of the Deputy Heads drafted a working paper to show how the scheme might work in practice and a staff committee was set up to look into the implications of the scheme, but the opposition remained implacable. The NUT representative seemed to look upon it as a personal crusade to save his members' lunch hour; the staff committee reported back adversely and the teacher governors opposed the scheme when it came before the governors' meeting. In the end, the lunch hour was not changed and mutters were heard in the staffroom that this simply summed things up at Downfell High School. 'It's always the same here – there's a lot of talk and no action,' they said.

Brian had got everything wrong. His attempt to implement a fairly straightforward organisational change is an object lesson in how not to do it.

1   *His objectives were unclear*
No-one was sure what Brian wanted to achieve. If his aim was to deal with discipline problems occurring during the lunch hour by removing the opportunity for misbehaviour, he was dealing with a symptom, not the cause of the indiscipline. Whatever his intention really was, he gave staff the impression that he was acting on a whim.

2   *He didn't bother to prepare*

> *One of the biggest traps is* ... *the failure of organisational leaders to resist the temptation to rush through the planning process to get to the action stage.*
> (R Beckhard and RT Harris *Organisational Transition – Managing Complex Change,* 1977)

Brian didn't seem to think he needed to make any preparation. Cutting corners and skimping on the preparation time needed for change can be a recipe for disaster.

3 *There was a complete lack of consultation*

Brian began a new term by announcing that he wanted to change the structure of the school day. He does not seem to have consulted his senior staff and took the staff meeting totally by surprise. If you spring change on people without prior warning, you are asking for trouble. It makes them feel threatened and provokes their hostility to the plan. This happened at Downfell School, and invoked two immediate responses: 'What on earth does he want to do that for?' and 'We don't want this change.' You will usually have to deal with dynamic conservatism (ie resistance to any change and determination to continue with the familiar), Making people feel threatened only adds to your problems.

4 *No details of the plan were available*

This was partly because the details had not been worked out, and partly because Brian did not seem to think it was necessary to provide this kind of information. It meant that the teachers were unclear about how the scheme was meant to work. This made them suspicious and reluctant to co-operate. Their immediate reaction was to block the proposed scheme by raising every objection that they could think of.

It is usually a good idea to put out a working paper about a week before the meeting in which an important change is to be discussed, so that people can see what the issues are and think out the implications. It is always sensible to allow people to air their fears and to show them that you have taken the issues that they have raised into account in your planning.

5 *The scheme was owned only by Brian*

There was absolutely no support for this scheme. Had Brian insisted on implementing it in these circumstances, it would have been doomed to failure. Brian had not discussed the idea with anyone before he put it to the staff. When a staff committee was eventually set up, it could not see any advantages in making the change. This was because nobody really wanted it – or understood its purpose.

A useful rule of thumb is: An initiative planned and implemented top down is less likely to succeed than one that is owned and supported by the staff who have to carry it out.

6   *The staff did not respect the management*

The staff were not surprised at what happened. They thought it was typical of the way that the school was run. Brian was clearly not an effective manager and did not seem to be held in respect by his staff. Nor did they expect the senior management team to be able to do anything to make up for Brian's deficiences as a leader. Their expectation was that any scheme put forward by Brian and his senior management team would lack rigour, would be badly organised and would probably fail. This is an important reason why they did not give the plan the benefit of the doubt. Change generally works best and is easiest to implement in an organisation where past changes have been successful. In Downfell High School previous experience led to low expectations and Brian's task was made more difficult. Failing to get his scheme implemented when he had taken personal responsibility for its management, naturally further undermined confidence in Brian's leadership.

7   *The scheme failed to convince*

Brian communicated the scheme very badly at the staff meeting and signally failed to convince the staff that there were any advantages in adopting it. Because no thought had been given to the practicalities of the scheme, all kinds of problems emerged that had not been anticipated. Another reason why it failed to win acceptance was that the staff did not believe it would work.

8   *He hadn't thought through the implications*

The change, which sounded so simple, in fact affected everyone – staff, pupils, the dinner ladies etc. Brian did not seem to have given any thought to this aspect of the change and gave no reassurance to the people affected. What was the Drama teacher meant to do? If Brian had made arrangements for her he certainly didn't tell her what they were. No wonder people were so hostile to his plan!

He hadn't thought through the implications

Some factors affecting successful change
1 Change requires support and pressure.
2 Each change has two components – content and process.
3 Headteachers have the most important role in managing change.
4 Change needs to be communicated fully to those involved.
5 Teachers need to be convinced of the need for change.
6 Individual teachers need to take ownership of change.
7 Effective change needs clear plans and procedures.
8 Moving towards small, concrete goals works better than setting vast targets, no matter how desirable.
9 Each stage needs to be assimilated for the next to succeed.
10 Past experience of successful/unsuccessful change influences attitudes and expectations.
11 Change works best in an organisation which has been trained to accept change!

Case Study 3.2   *For reflection*
EXAMPLES FROM INDUSTRY

Characteristics of people who are good at handling change

1 They know clearly what they want to achieve.
2 They can translate desires into practical action.
3 They can see proposed changes not only from their own viewpoint but also from that of others.
4 They don't mind being out on a limb.
5 They show irreverence for tradition, but respect for experience.
6 They plan flexibly, matching constancy of ends against a repertoire of available means.
7 They are not discouraged by setbacks.
8 They harness circumstances to enable change to be implemented.
9 They clearly explain change.
10 They involve their staff in the management of change and protect their security.
11 They don't pile one change on top of another.
12 They present change as a rational decision.
13 They make change personally rewarding for people wherever possible.
14 They share maximum information about possible outcomes.
15 They show that change is 'related to the business'.
16 They have a history of successful change behind them.

Rosemary Stewart *Change – the Challenge for Management* McGraw-Hill, 1983.

The Rank Xerox Management of Change Model

Change management
Stage 1: Prioritising
What are your major task priorities?
How do these tasks link with other things going on in school?
What timescale is involved in your priority tasks?
Which task needs doing most urgently?

Stage 2: Clarifying

What is the hoped-for outcome of this change?
What specific **objectives** must you set to achieve this outcome?
What is the main **target group** for the change?
Which other groups will be affected by any of your actions?
Who needs to be involved in decision making and action?

Stage 3: Creating

Identify your potential resources – what factors will help you gain your objectives?
What factors may **hinder** you in gaining your objectives?
Generate alternatives – what are *all* your possible courses of action?
Which courses of action are the most viable?
How should the best alternative be selected?

Stage 4: Formulating

At this planning stage you should consider questions such as:
Resourcing – How will this change be resourced? Time? Cost? People?
Influencing – Who has got to be won over? How?
Acting/delegating – What specific actions do you need to take? Who should be responsible for specific actions?
Prioritising – What is your timetable for action? Which are the priority actions? How do any actions mesh with your existing commitments?

Stage 5: Implementing

Is the planning stage now complete?
Are the targets and timetable clear, understood, and realistic?
Commitment – how can you gain and maintain the commitment of all the people involved in the change?
Communication – is your plan visible, and have your intentions been communicated to everyone who is affected?
How will communications be maintained while your actions continue?
Monitoring/control – how will your actions be co-ordinated and monitored, and by whom?

Stage 6: Reviewing

The reviewing process will take place both during the change, and after the change has been implemented.

Targets – are the targets for your actions at each stage clear and unambiguous?

How are you going to review your progress against the agreed targets?

Evaluation – how are you going to evaluate the impact of the change?

Who is the best person to make an objective evaluation?

How can your experience best be made available to others?

4 Managing the pastoral system

I could scarcely believe how bad it was ...
(Derek Farr, the new Pastoral Deputy at Bestwick Park, was
confiding to another of the school's Deputies, Mike Wade)

*The image of the school under Mrs Gatlin is of a flourishing,
go-ahead place involved in all the current initiatives, but the
pastoral system was like another world. Of course Fred Brown,
the previous Deputy, had been in post a long time. He was
extremely authoritarian and hostile to most of the recent developments in education. Mrs Gatlin tells me that when she first came,
she asked him to introduce a PSE programme, but he simply
wouldn't co-operate and she decided that as Fred was nearing the
end of his career, she would sit it out. She says she preferred to
wait and have it done properly than force Fred into implementing
reforms that he did not understand.*

*It is not just a matter of introducing PSE, which is difficult
enough at any time. Although Fred was authoritarian, I suspect
that in the last few years he had just let go. There is no uniformity
whatsoever, no real system or records. Fred personally scared the
pants off everyone in the establishment, pupils and staff alike, so
everyone avoided him, which he seems to have taken as a sign*

that everything was OK. On the rare occasions when he held Year Heads' meetings, there was never apparently any real discussion. Fred barked out a few orders and everyone went off and did their own thing. Year group meetings appear to have been held regularly, but if any minutes were kept of these meetings, no-one bothered to send them to Fred. Although there are some very good individuals – Sunitti Pattni, for example, is doing a splendid job – some of the year heads have got into bad habits or are ineffective. Discipline is poor, largely because it is not properly enforced. Punctuality is a problem, there is some truancy from lessons and some children are regularly out of uniform. The pupils know that they can get away with things, and excel at playing one teacher off against another.

Mrs Gatlin says that major changes are urgently needed in the pastoral system and after only a short time here I totally concur with her opinion. The question that is really bothering me, is how I should approach trying to improve the system. I am very new to senior management and to the school. Mrs Gatlin is expecting a lot of me; I don't want to disappoint her ...

What would you advise Derek to do in this situation?

Case Study 4.2   *For reflection*
**APPLYING MANAGEMENT TECHNIQUES
TO THE PASTORAL SYSTEM AT
BESTWICK PARK: THE PROBLEM-
SOLVING MODEL**

Derek was new to his post and clearly rather daunted by the size and complexity of the task he faced. It was difficult for him to distinguish the wood from the trees, and to know where he should start. He was anxious in case the Head would be disappointed if he didn't take immediate action and worried that there would be a lot of opposition to any changes he might make. He discussed his troubles with his colleague, Mike Wade.

Mike reminded him that Mrs Gatlin would not have appointed him to the deputy headship if she did not think he had the potential to manage the job. He also pointed out that although Mike was inexperienced as a manager, there was no need to reinvent the wheel. Mike knew from his own experience how quickly management skills could be learnt. There were plenty of management techniques that Derek could use to help him. From the possible models, Derek selected the *Problem-solving model* as he felt it would help him to analyse the issues and generate some possible solutions.

The problem-solving model

1 Clarification
- What is the problem?
- Does it have component parts?
- What are the current symptoms?

2 Analysis
- Diagnose the problem
- Categorise the symptoms
- Suggest possible causes
- Consider the viewpoints of different people concerned

3 Approaches
- Generate ideas for solution
- What are the possible strategies?
- Who can help with solution?

4 Action
- What can be done – in the short term and longer term?
- Specify steps to deal with problem
- Who is going to monitor progress?

What follows shows what happened when Derek and Mike applied the problem-solving model.

1 Clarification
- *What is the problem?* The Pastoral system needs to be over-hauled. It is not operating effectively.
- *Does it have component parts?*
  The pastoral system needs an overhaul
  PSE has never been introduced

The year tutors do not function as a team
They largely ignored the previous leader

- *What are the symptoms?* Poor discipline, reflected in poor punctuality, lack of uniform and some truancy. Pupils are getting away with things.

2 Analyse the issues

- Derek will have to establish himself as a leader. How he deals with reforming the pastoral system will be a test of Derek as a senior manager.
- He has to create a team from a number of individuals who have been in post for several years.
- He has to impose some kind of structure upon the pastoral system.

3 Approaches – generate ideas and suggest possible strategies

a) *Strategies for improving the system:*

- *Do a systems analysis* Derek needs to stand back from the situation and analyse what the problems are and what is causing them. He has already started to think about the deficiencies of the present system, so he has started this stage.
- *Decide his objectives* If Derek does not like what currently exists, he has to have something better to offer. He will have been appointed because Mrs Gatlin thought he had the creativity and capacity to deal with a complex and sensitive task. His aim will be to create an effective pastoral system; to determine his objectives he will have to establish what elements he considers a good pastoral system should include. He has to analyse what these are and work out how they fit into a system. Some elements might be – an improved discipline system; the staged introduction of PSE; a profiling system; a system of recording lateness and absence from lessons.
- *Decide what the stages/phases should be and who should be involved* The difficult thing with a large and complicated task is to decide where to start. Derek cannot do everything immediately and Mrs Gatlin will not expect instant delivery of a completely revamped pastoral system, but she will expect him to be able to tell her where he is going to start; what the timetable will be and who is going to be involved. There is no need for him to do everything himself, and in fact trying to do so could be counterproductive, but if he is going to set up a

working party or task group he has first to clarify who is going to be in it, what its terms of reference are to be, when and how it is to report back and to whom.

- *Produce a development plan* Derek needs to draft a development paper for the pastoral system.

  How to draft a development paper is fully dealt with in another chapter, but briefly he should divide it into 5 sections;
    i Where are we now? (An analysis (brief and tactful) of the current position and why change is needed.)
    ii Where do we want to go? (His ideas for an improved system.)
    iii How are we going to get there? (The timetable of change and methods of implementation.)
    iv What are the resource implications? (The costs may determine the pace of change.)
    v How do we know when we have arrived? (Suggestions for monitoring and evaluating the new system.)

  Derek is initiating an overhaul of a major section of the school; it needs to be carefully planned and phased. Most development plans cover three years. The development plan is Derek's programme and should serve as the basis for future negotiation.

b) *Strategies for developing the team:*

To get his ideas accepted by the Year Heads who will be important implementers of his policies, Derek will need to do some team building.

- *Build on good practice where possible* Some Year Heads were unilaterally doing good work. (It should be possible to incorporate some of their ideas into the new system. Sunitti Pattni, for example, was operating a system where she monitored lateness to lessons, unexplained absences and uniform. This could easily be extended to all the year groups.) It would be wise, however, for Derek to adopt ideas from more than one Year Head, to prevent any suggestion of favouritism.
- *Involve the Year Heads* It was unlikely that the Year Heads were really blind to the problem. More likely they had given up with Fred and they were afraid that Derek would blame them for the deficiencies of the pastoral system. Talking it through with them could reveal what they thought and indicate how many allies or enemies he was likely to have.

He would also need to arrange sessions with individual Year Heads. People do not always talk freely when they are in groups, and no-one had given the members of this team any real attention for years.

- *Change the format of the meetings*   One of the problems had been that Fred's meetings were really only briefing sessions, there had never been any discussion. It does not mean that the Year Heads do not *want* to talk. Derek needs to change the format of the meetings by introducing an agenda, discussion and minutes. (An example of action minutes can be found later in this chapter.)
- *Use analysis techniques to assess the potential of the team*   There are materials that Derek could use to analyse the roles played by the individuals in his team and the way team members interact. These materials were developed for industry, but educationalists are increasingly making use of them. The most popular is the questionnaire devised by Meredith Belbin to analyse team roles.

  Derek may meet with initial resistance to the questionnaire, but he should endeavour to overcome this resistance. Once people use this exercise they generally enjoy it and become fascinated by the results – their own and other people's. Using team analysis can reveal hidden talents and help the team-building process.

- *Make the Year Heads the nucleus of the working party*   If the development plan is purely Derek's creation it will be a 'top down' imposed change; resistance is then likely to be much greater than if the staff are involved in formulating the policy. The support of the Year Heads is crucial to the success of the development and it would be insulting to them if any planning group is set up that did not at least include several of them. They need to be consulted about what form the planning group should take and what proportion of it should be formed from the pastoral team.
- *Provide Inset for the team and individuals*   This will help to build up expertise. Inset was not likely to have been a priority of Fred's and providing training could be a bonus of the new regime. The Year Heads will certainly need some Inset before they start to develop PSE. Some might appreciate a chance to improve their counselling skills, or knowledge about drugs or child abuse, others might benefit from the opportunity to

do a middle management course, if one is available. Derek himself probably needs to go on a management course that deals with team building.

It may prove possible for Derek and the Year Heads to go to a hotel, college or industrial training centre for an Inset weekend. This would facilitate teambuilding while allowing the team to focus on the central issue of developing the pastoral system.

c) *Strategies for establishing himself as a leader*
- *Be pro-active* Derek has to take the initiative or the situation will get away from him. Some of the ideas generated to identify a strategy and build up the team will actually help Derek establish himself eg setting up and leading the working party will certainly demonstrate his leadership skills.
- *Monitor the system* Changing the format of the Year Head meetings will help Derek keep control of the pastoral system in a way that Fred clearly did not attempt. Regular sessions with the team and individuals will help him assert himself. He has the right to expect regular agenda and minutes from year group meetings and may want to sample some of these meetings. He might also want to set some performance indicators eg by getting a Year Head to monitor one aspect of a year group, such as lateness to lessons.
- *Be firm but fair* Derek has to demonstrate that he is aware of current practices and that he is not prepared to tolerate bad habits. How he deals with the case of the Year Head who is using his pastoral role as an excuse to absent himself from his Biology classes, will be watched by the whole staff, not just the Year Heads.
- *Provide encouragement and support* There is a lot of good practice already in progress. Derek should show clearly that he intends to build on it and appreciates the sterling work that is being done. The Year Heads seem to have received very little encouragement or support in the last few years.

d) *Who can help with the solution?*
- *The Head* Mrs Gatlin clearly wants changes in the pastoral system, so Derek should be able to expect some help from her. To get her support he must brief her clearly about his analysis of the position and his proposals. If he has definite

suggestions to make and is clear where he needs support, he is likely to make a much better impression on her than if he looks to her to provide all the ideas; this will also help him secure the resources he needs in addition to personal support. If she is vehemently opposed to a part of his plan, he should seriously consider whether it is worth pursuing, as the Head's support is crucial to his success.

- *The Pastoral Adviser* The LEA usually has an Adviser/ Inspector with responsibility for the pastoral system and the school normally has an attached adviser. To discuss the problem and possible solutions with either of these advisers could help Derek.
- *Colleagues in similar positions in neighbouring schools* Visiting or talking to other Pastoral Deputies in the area could help Derek. They may have had to tackle similar problems.
- *Some training for Derek* Some LEAs provide an induction foundation course for Deputy Heads and this could be generally beneficial. More specifically, training which centres on team building could be very useful indeed. The Adviser could probably tell him what is available.

4   Action
Some aspects of the problem need to be tackled immediately, others are clearly more long-term. Derek's first step should be to prioritise them, sorting out the long from the short-term solutions.
- The first component of the problem – the need to establish himself as a leader – would seem to be both urgent and important. Derek should immediately start to apply the solutions he worked out to this problem.
- Some training for Derek would also seem to be a priority as this would help to develop him as a leader.

It is less urgent to make immediate changes to the pastoral system. Rushing into action, ill-prepared and with inadequate consultation and support, would make a bad impression on Mrs Gatlin. This is the last thing that Derek would want to happen.

What he has to do is establish an effective framework for development. This means setting up a working party and constructing a development plan that gives the deadlines for the stages of the programme and sets out the areas and issues to be considered. The plan would provide the agenda for change, the working party's task would be to make detailed proposals. Leading a working party would serve several purposes: it would demonstrate Derek's ability as a leader, help with team building for the Year Heads and give staff the opportunity to contribute to decisions about what should go into the system.

Case Study 4.3   *For action*
**APPLYING MANAGEMENT TECHNIQUES:
TASK MANAGEMENT**

1 Prioritising
What needs doing most urgently?
How does this mesh with other things going on?
What time-scale are we working to?

2 Clarification
What is the hoped for outcome?
What are the specific objectives to achieve this outcome?
How do these objectives mesh with other things going on?
What would be affected by any actions?
Who is the primary target group?
Who are the secondary targets?
Who needs to be involved in decision making and action?

3 Creation
Identify the potential resources – what factors will help gain the objectives?
What are the hindering factors?
Generating alternatives – what are all the possible courses of action?
Which are the most viable?
Selection – how should the best alternative be selected?

4 Formulating
Resourcing   How will this action be resourced? Who? Time? Cost?

Influencing   Who has got to be won over? How?

Acting   What specific actions do we need to take?

Delegating   Who should be involved in actions?

Prioritising   What is the timetable for action? Which are the priority actions? How does this action mesh with existing commitments?

Contingencies   What are the contingency plans? What are the contingency triggers?

5 Implementation

Is the planning stage now complete?

Are the targets and timetable clear and realistic?

How can we gain and maintain the commitment of all the people involved?

Communication – is the plan visible? Have our intentions been communicated to everyone who is affected?

How will communications be maintained while the actions continue?

Monitoring/controlling – how will actions be monitored? By whom?

What are the key indicators of success/failure?

6 Evaluation

How will the action be evaluated? Who is the best person to make an objective evaluation?

How can our experience best be made available to others?

For action

Apply the Task Management Model to the pastoral problem at Bestwick Park. Compare the results with those of the *Problem-solving model* in Case Study 4.1.

You will find that quite often there are a variety of approaches you can apply to the same situation and you will have to choose between them. You should choose the one with which you feel most comfortable; do not worry about departing from the model or supplementing it as and when you think appropriate. Management models are planning aids available for your use, tools to help you clarify your thoughts.

Case Study 4.4   *For reflection*
APPLYING MANAGEMENT TECHNIQUES:
FORCE FIELD ANALYSIS

One of Derek's aims at this stage should be to identify possible resources that will help him achieve the outcome he wants. Resources in this context means anything that he can use to help him – people, ideas, time, physical resources, influence. One approach to identifying both positive and negative resources, is to use a process called Force Field Analysis. This technique is often used by managers of change as it helps to focus their thoughts.

Like brainstorming, force field analysis is best done in a group, using a large sheet of paper or the board so that people can see ideas being developed.

1 Identify the 'ideal solution' you want to move towards, and write this at the top of the sheet.
2 Identify any possible resource which could help move towards your ideal result. These are your *driving forces*. Write these on the driving force side of your sheet. You do not need to go into too much detail at this stage – indeed you might brainstorm to generate a wide range of ideas on driving forces.
3 Now go through a similar process to identify all the possible *resisting forces*, which are the elements which could work against your achieving the change towards your ideal situation.
4 Once you have identified all possible driving and resisting forces, go back to analyse them in more detail. Try to assess the relative importance of each force – make the length or the width of each line roughly proportional to the strength of the force.

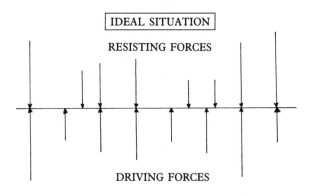

5   What are the key driving forces? What can you plan to do to maximise their effect?
6   What are the key resisting forces? How can you plan to minimise or eliminate their effects?

This is what happened when Derek, helped by Michael Wade, applied Force Field Analysis to the Pastoral System:

Force field analysis

Ideal situation: an effective pastoral system

Driving forces

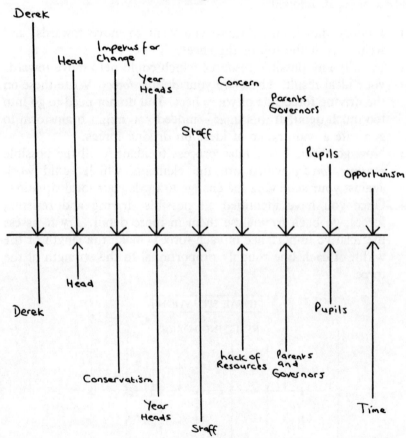

Resisting forces

Note that some of the forces appear on both sides. This is because they are potential driving forces if they can be harnessed, but they also have the potential to be resistances. The Head is one such example: her support is crucial for achieving success, but if she does not approve of Derek's plans or his methods of carrying them out, she could block all progress. Derek's next step will be to try to work out how to build on the driving forces and to minimise the resisting forces so that he can implement change successfully.

Case Study 4.5   *For discussion*
LEARNING FROM COLLEAGUES:
REWARDS AND SANCTIONS

As well as using management models, Derek could also learn a lot from talking to colleagues, who have had to deal with the same kind of problem as he now faced. Mike suggested that Derek should visit Mary Phillips, who was an old friend of his and the pastoral deputy at a school in a neighbouring LEA. It was an opportunity for Derek to discuss with Mary how she had tackled reforming the pastoral system in a fairly similar school. One of the items that Mary showed Derek was the paper she had drawn up on 'Rewards and Sanctions'. This could provide a model for him from which he could draft a paper on 'Discipline'. She talked through with him how she had set about the task.

First I had a long session with the Year Heads and we discussed what we wanted to achieve. It became clear that one of the problems for our school was that although we seemed to have a lot of sanctions, there seemed to be very few rewards. The Year Heads suspected that the pupils did not feel valued. We discussed the problem at our Year Heads' meeting, then I wrote a paper which aimed to change and improve this situation. You will see that I dealt with rewards before sanctions. The draft paper was then discussed at another Year Heads' meeting and some amendments were made. Then it was distributed to the whole staff about a week before the next long staff meeting. It was the main discussion item for that staff meeting and provoked a lot of valuable contributions.

It was amended to include some of these ideas, adopted as school policy and it was introduced at the beginning of the following term. No one could say that there had not been a full consultation period or that it was not clear what the policy was. Now I am monitoring how it is working and I am pleased with progress so far, as people seem to be making a real effort to make it work and the pupils seem to value the commendations.

Mary's paper on Rewards and Sanctions can be found in Chapter 7 Communications – Drafting a document.

For discussion
1   What factors do you think contributed to Mary's success in reforming the pastoral system in her school?
2   How might Derek apply the approach used by Mary to his own situation?

Case Study 4.6   *For reflection*
MONITORING THE SYSTEM

Mike Wade also suggested to Derek some mechanisms by which he could control and monitor the pastoral system without appearing officious.

1   Action minutes
Previously, the Year Heads did not provide the Deputy Head with any feedback from their year meetings or any indication of what was happening in their year group. One way in which Derek could approach this problem is to use Action Minutes. If he introduces this system for both his own and their meetings, it will provide a uniform approach while keeping the amount of paper work to the minimum. It shows the format of a meeting clearly, allows individual members of the year group to take responsibility for individual items and records decisions taken. This will give Derek an indication of the concerns of a particular year group and he can follow this up with individual sessions with the Year Heads.

Fuller minutes may sometimes be necessary if the whole meeting is devoted to discussing a major issue such as discipline, where it is felt that a record of the discussion is needed.

AGENDA FOR A YEAR HEADS' MEETING

Timing	Item	Who	Action
30m	Assembly	Sunitti Pattni (3rd Year)	1 Talk to tutors about improving arrival time to ensure prompt start.
			2 At year meeting discuss idea of increasing no. of assemblies led by pupils.
			3 Investigate possibility of producing own hymn book. Mrs Pattni to talk to Head of RE.
10m	Lost Property	Nigel North (4th Year)	Hold kit check in form time Thursday.
15m	Letter of complaint from parent	Deputy Head	Points noted, also DH's reply. Try to improve liaison with Matron so that we all know about any incident.
15m	Individual. All pupil concerns		Mainly information. Cherry Sparks to go on YH report for 1 week.
	AOB		Information about 3rd Year Charity Activities.

2 The weekly record sheet

When she became Head of Year, Sunitti Pattni had devised a scheme for monitoring her year group's latenesses, absences etc by using a very simple weekly record sheet. The system had been in operation for over a year and had found favour with her year team because it was a clear and effective way of recording and communicating important data.

TUTOR GROUP		WEEK COMMENCING	
Name	No. of lates	Name	No. of lates
1		11	
2		12	
3		13	
4		14	
5		15	
6		16	
7		17	
8		18	
9		19	
10		20	
Name	Uniform/Equipment	Name	Uniform/Equipment
1		11	
2		12	
3		13	
4		14	
5		15	
6		16	
7		17	
8		18	
9		19	
10		20	
Name	Unexplained absence(no note)	Name	Unexplained absence (no note)
1		11	
2		12	
3		13	
4		14	
5		15	
6		16	
7		17	
8		18	
9		19	
10		20	

Derek could extend to other year groups a system which was already operating successfully in one section of the school. In this way he can easily build up a record of what is happening in the pastoral system and this will provide him with the basis of a system for monitoring its progress.

It should also be fairly easy for him to apply performance indicators, eg *Attendance*. Each class should have an average attendance objective throughout the Winter or Spring terms of 85% or better.

Case Study 4.7   *For action*
DEREK FARR'S PASTORAL CASEBOOK

1 The reluctant tutor

Note from John Hayward, Head of the Second Year to Derek
Farr, Deputy Head Pastoral:

DEAR DEREK

I'd like your advice on a matter that has
been worrying me for some time now. It's about
Brian Dee. As you know, he is quite an able
teacher, enthusiastic about his own subject and —
according to his Head of Department - conscientious
about his marking and other duties. But he
is not at all conscientious as a tutor, and is
always finding reasons why he should not
be with his tutor group.

As you know, we have to use every
available full-time member of staff to have
enough tutors to cover all the form groups, so
he can't just opt out of having a tutor
group. Some of the second year have been
trying it on recently — when I dealt with them
I noticed that a number of the miscreants
were from Brian's tutor group. How should I
approach the situation?

How should Derek deal with the reluctant tutor and the situation
that is developing in Brian Dee's tutor group? Formulate Derek's
reply to John Hayward.

2 Role conflict

Note from Simon Tucker, Head of the Science Faculty to Derek Farr, Pastoral Deputy:

```
Dear Derek,

I hesitate to add to your problems, as I remember what it
was like when I first came last year, but I feel that I
should bring to your attention the fact that Nigel North
may be a hard-working Year Head, but it is very much at
the expense of his role as a teacher of Biology. My main
concern is not how little Nigel is contributing to his
department, though I am worried about the overload that
Christopher Jones, as Head of Biology, is having to
carry, but that, quite simply, Nigel is absent from his
classroom all too frequently.

When I raised the matter with him, he claimed that as
Head of Year, he is expected to deal with every crisis
immediately it occurs. If this is really the procedure,
I must say that I totally disagree with it, and would
suggest that it comes under review as soon as possible.

My immediate concern is that pupils are not being taught,
and Nigel has both GCSE and A level sets. It is not good
enough to leave sixth formers on their own while he goes
off to deal with pastoral problems. They need teaching
just as much as junior forms, and he has the juniors
covered often enough - I frequently find a non-specialist
supply teacher covering his class when I go to Nigel's
room.

Could you clarify the position, please, as I am not
prepared to allow this unsatisfactory situation to
continue. I am amazed that there have been no complaints
from parents. When can we discuss this matter? I should
like it resolved as soon as possible.
```

What policy should Derek as Manager of the Pastoral System follow with Simon Tucker, the Head of Science and Nigel North, the Head of Fourth Year?

3 Record keeping

FROM: Derek Farr, Deputy Head, Pastoral
TO: All Year Heads

You may be aware that some problems arose on a recent Fourth Form History expedition. When the incident was brought to my knowledge and I needed full information about the main trouble-maker, I found that the pupil's record card was almost bare of information. Yet when I began to discuss this pupil with the teachers involved in the incident, they claimed that Jackie Street was always in trouble and told me of a number of previous incidents in which she had been the ringleader. This led me to examine the record card system for that year group and I found that most cards have very little information indeed. I suspect this is probably true of other year groups, not just the Fourth Year.

I am rather concerned about the way that we keep records. If a serious incident occurred and the Head asked me for information so that she could recommend the governors to suspend Jackie or a similar pupil, I should have no cumulative record of her previous offences, the number of staff involved, or previous sanctions.

I should be interested in your comments and feel that we should air this matter thoroughly at the next Heads of Year meeting next week.

What are the chief ingredients of a successful record system in relation to 'difficult' pupils?

How do you think Derek, as manager of the school's pastoral system, should approach the problem of inadequate pupil records?

Apply any of the management models illustrated earlier in this chapter to solving these problems.

5 Managing time

7.45: Arrive. Post cover arrangements for the day. Clear noticeboards of out-of-date information. *Administration/Clerical*
7.50: Have coffee – breakfast. *Personal*
7.50–8.30: Man phone till secretary arrives, taking messages eg about staff absence and deal with additional cover. *Administration/Clerical*
7.55–8.00: See Caretaker about likely arrival of plumbers to deal with damp in new building and what the room change implications would be. *Management*
8.00–8.10: Sort out some materials for duplication for use with A Level class. *Teaching preparation*
8.10–8.35: See 2nd and 3rd Form tutors as they arrive to find out their preferred times for profiling sessions at the end of the month. *Management/Administration*
8.35–8.50: Mainly in staffroom talking to staff. *Management*
8.50–9.05: Attend Assembly. *Teaching*
9.05–9.45: Work out possible rooms in which to hold profiling sessions. Type arrangements for the profiling sessions into the computer. Print it out and give print-out to office for duplication. On cover sheet work out cover demands for the session. Telephone two supply teachers, book them for the session and cover the rest with staff. *Administration*
9.45–9.50: Go to office. Discuss work schedule over next week. *Administration/Management*
9.50–10.10: See a HOD who took up post at start of this term. Staff development – induction process. *Management*
10.10–10.20: Session with the Head. Go through calendar for

the rest of term and check organisational needs. Discuss Architect's visit later in the day and implications of plumbing problems. Discuss problem about a pupil. *Management*

10.20–10.40: Break. See pupil – sent by Matron. Go to staffroom and talk to relevant staff about result of discussion with Caretaker. *Management*

10.40–11.55: Teach A Level Upper Sixth. *Teaching*

11.55–12.25: Dinner duty in the Dining Hall.

12.25–12.55: Chair staff working party meeting – Marketing Committee. *Management*

12.55–1.00: See pupil with personal problem. *Management*

1.00–1.05: Have lunch. *Personal*

1.05–1.35: Go to see Technology Manager – lengthy discussion about future development of Technology. *Curriculum development/ Management*

1.35–2.00: Session with Head. Discuss department development plans, school management plan and some implications of LMS. *Management*

2.00–2.15: Check following day's cover arrangements. *Administration*

Visitor arrives – teaching project researcher. *Teaching*

2.15–3.30: Teach 5th. GCSE Lesson taped by researcher. *Teaching/Inset*

3.30–5.00: Curriculum Working Party meeting. *Curriculum development/Management*

5.10: Go home. *Personal*

Figure 3   *A Deputy's day*

The timetable of a Deputy's day (Figure 3) highlights a number of features about the nature of the job:

1   The long hours – the Deputy spends over 9 hours at the workplace on a normal day. (The timetable does not include work done at home later.)

2   The fragmented day – Charles Handy has commented that when he observed school senior managers they were never able to have a long period of time engaged on one task. The day runs in short bursts of time and the deputy has to be able to switch from one issue or problem to another and deal with them rapidly and effectively.

3   The amount of teaching done – The Deputy taught half the day, four out of eight teaching periods and all examination teaching. S/he was not late for a lesson nor prevented from teaching it by any organisational crisis. Was this luck or good management?

4   The level of activity – It was a typically busy day. There were meetings in the lunch hour and after school. Lunch was a quick five minutes some time after the start of afternoon school.

5   The Deputy has broken down the day's tasks into categories – personal (eg have lunch), clerical, administrative, management, teaching and Inset. Although there has been much criticism of Deputies as highly-paid clerical officers, management features highly on this list.

6   Several items on the list did deal with administration – sorting out cover, making arrangements for profiling sessions, organising room changes necessitated by problems of damp and the arrival of the plumbers. It adds up to about 1 hour 20 minutes, mainly in the early part of the morning, and indicates the manner in which keeping the school running smoothly has to be worked into a Deputy Head's day.

7   There are a lot of fairly short meetings with different people; some of these meetings deal with strategic issues such as curriculum development.

8   The two meetings with the Head are different in nature. In the morning administrative matters form the core of the discussion, in the afternoon management issues about future planning. This indicates clear thinking.

9   The Deputy went to the staff room twice to talk to staff and to communicate developments. Communication is a vital part of his/her management task. It is important that the Deputy does not remain isolated in his/her office.

10   There was no slack or spare time – every available moment seems to be occupied, yet this is not a diary of crisis management. The sessions with teachers and the head seemed to have been pre-arranged and on this particular day there were no interruptions to deal with disruptive pupils or a domestic disaster. Contingency plans were made to cope with the plumbers needing access to some rooms, but the Deputy was able to spend much of the day on forward planning. If a crisis had occurred, some of these sessions could have been re-arranged.

This extract from a Deputy Head's day helps to illustrate some essential management skills for a successful senior manager:

- *Interpersonal skills*
- *Communications skills*
- *Organisational/administrative skills*

It also illustrates that the successful senior manager must be an expert manager of *Time*.

A guide to effective management of time

1 Be proactive rather than reactive

A good manager of time always plans ahead. S/he is in control of the situation, not merely reacting to events. S/he should know what s/he wants to achieve in a given amount of time. Some of us naturally complete tasks quickly, others of us are slow but steady. If you are one of the second type you have to watch that you do not let things get on top of you. Whichever type you are, careful planning will make you more effective.

2 Prioritise

The demands made on a senior manager may seem endless, but some of the jobs are much more important than others. This means that you should prioritise them, ie put them in an order of merit. Ask yourself:

- What are *the most important* things?
- What are *the most urgent* things?

We make no excuses for repeating this principle – it is so crucial to succeeding as a manager.

Urgent tasks are the things that have to be sorted out now, eg there has been a flood overnight and some room changes are needed. If the pupils are not given the right information in time, they will try to go to their normal rooms. This will cause chaos and both staff and pupils will be annoyed. You cannot put off telling the pupils about the disaster until next week when you have some spare time. A flood is both urgent and important.

Some things will have high priority because they are urgent; however they may not be very important. Other tasks may be extremely important for the school, but they may not need doing today or even this week, eg making decisions about next year's Inset. You should try to list and categorise the tasks. Use **U** for urgent and **P** or **HP** for high priority. Some tasks will be both **U** and **HP**. They will clearly come high on your list.

3   Always work within your deadline

When you make your priorities list always work out when the job has to be finished. You want to make sure that you meet the deadline. To do the job properly you need to give yourself time to think. You cannot draft an evaluation paper or an Inset proposal without thinking carefully about its structure. A rush job usually shows. Shoddy work does not earn you respect, nor can you expect other people to meet the deadlines that you set if you cannot work to time yourself. A good manager has the job complete with some time to spare. Remember when you set your own deadline to take into account that you may need the office to type or duplicate your proposals. Remember, too, that many of the arrangements that you have to make are most successful if they are completed and communicated two or three weeks in advance.

4   Have a system for dealing with the trivia

Do not become a slave to the tryanny of the urgent! Ticking off lists of completed trivia is a false satisfaction. It is, however, worth making a little time at the beginning of each day to clear out of the way as many small tasks as possible. Decide how much time you are allotting to this. Do not let it take over and try not to let the tasks become urgent.

5   Keep your desk clear

File it or throw it – what is important is that you decide how you are going to deal with all the paper that accumulates on your desk. Keep your desk clear. A cluttered and untidy desk will not convince people that you are an effective manager. They will not believe that you know where anything is or that you have read their urgent request.

Keep your desk clear

6 Focus on the job in hand

You need to develop good powers of concentration as you have to work in short spans of time, with frequent interruptions. Work where you have to consult other people must be fitted into your school day as you cannot take this home. Drafting working papers will mainly need to be done at home as there are normally too many interruptions and too little free time during the school day to get anything worthwhile done. Wherever the work is done, what matters is that you give it your full attention so that you use the available time effectively.

One way of making a job more manageable is to break a substantial task down into its component parts, so that a major job becomes a series of smaller jobs with which you can deal step-by-step.

7 Do not procrastinate

A poor manager of time keeps putting off doing the job until s/he is always engaged in brinkmanship. This may be because:

- the task is dull and tedious so you put off doing it;
- it is difficult or lengthy and you don't fancy starting it now;
- it is not urgent; you could do it tomorrow or next week;
- you're not clear how you should tackle it so you convince yourself not to start yet, in case you get it wrong.

All these are excuses for not tackling a task. 'Do not put off for tomorrow what you can do today.' We support the Duke of Wellington's time-tested dictum, and would add: 'If you do, there will only be more work tomorrow.' (see Figure 4).

Procrastination
- Schedule the difficult – the important – the unpleasant tasks first
  Then follow your schedule
- Set deadlines
  'Go public' by announcing them
- Set acceptable standards but avoid perfectionism
  Perfection is unattainable
- Handle a task just once
  When you pick it up dispose of it
- Develop a philosophy about mistakes that will help you learn from them
- Reward yourself after the job is done

Remember
The average manager delays action on 60% of those daily in-tray items which could have been disposed of on first handling.

Originally reproduced from *MacKensie on Time* R Alec MacKensie, AMACOM, 1979

Figure 4

---

8   Use your diary or planner

If you are not good at time management, some form of personal organiser or diary could be a useful aid. Decide what form this planner should take – there is no 'best' type. Whether you use colour coding, columns for priorities, separate pages for each day or monthly calendar pages is very much a matter of personal preference. Remember that more than one diary can be a recipe for disaster! Your diary needs to be small enough to be on the desk, or visible on the wall, so that you can refer to it when fixing appointments.

You are likely to have a lot of meetings and visits from staff, parents, advisers etc. Make appointments at times convenient to your schedule: make sure you leave enough time between meetings and avoid becoming double-booked. You will make a very poor impression on a visitor if you keep checking the clock and cannot concentrate because you have fixed too many meetings or failed to leave sufficient time between them – or, even worse, if two visitors arrive to see you at the same time!

9   Avoid interruption if possible

If you really need to get a job done then it is important to ensure that you are not interrupted. Schedule the time for yourself and keep to it. Close your door. Get an 'engaged' sign and put it outside your door. Take the phone off the hook and arrange with the secretary that for this amount of time s/he will take messages for you. If the worst comes to the worst, evacuate your office and find somewhere else where you can work without interruption. But if you go off the premises, make sure that the Head and the office know where you are! Be ruthless because this will only work if you make it clear to people that you do mean it. Do not do this too frequently – but if you learn to be a good manager of time you will not need to use this technique very often.

10   Do not take on too many jobs

All the new initiatives have added to everyone's workload, not least that of the Deputy Head. As new jobs arise, they tend to be tacked onto your existing workload, which can make it increasingly unmanageable.

Remember that your school's development plan should include a periodic review of its senior managers' functions. Try to use this as an opportunity to ensure an even distribution of responsibilities. You won't be helping the school or yourself if you take on so many tasks that you cannot cope.

Case Study 5.1   *For action*
TIME MANAGEMENT

It is Thursday 23 March. You are Yvonne Perkins, Deputy Head
at Bestwick Park High School. You have just arrived at school.
You know that you have a busy day ahead and that there is an
important curriculum committee meeting at the end of the day.
As you hang up your coat, your mind ranges over the tasks and
meetings that you want to fit in today if possible.

The timechart will show you the structure of your day. It is also
your working sheet.

Part 1:
These are the tasks that you want to fit in:

1   You have drafted a working paper for this evening's meeting.
    You are worried because it has not yet reappeared from the
    office. It will need checking and circulating. If it is not ready
    in time, you will have to make some OHPs.
2   Because of his bad behaviour, Terry Dene had been referred to
    senior detention, which you took last night. Terry did not turn
    up. You need to take some action.
3   You want to have a talk with the Inset Co-ordinator, because
    the school's Inset bid has to be completed by Monday in order
    to get to the LEA by the deadline date. He has been asking to
    see you all week.
4   You have some 5th year coursework that you have not yet
    graded because you have been busy with your curriculum
    paper. It is almost the end of term and you ought to give
    them their grades.
5   You want to see the office quite urgently. You suspect that it
    is not only your curriculum paper that has failed to materialise.
    How overloaded is the office?
6   The Head has asked you to fit in a session sometime before
    this evening's meeting. She will be out from 11 am to about
    2.30 pm.
7   A session with a teacher who joined the school this term has
    had to be postponed because of her absence. It is part of her
    induction process, can you fit it in today? She is free period 4.

Use column 1 to see how many of these items you can fit into Yvonne's day.

Time management sheet Yvonne Perkins' day

TIME	1	2	3
8-00	Arrive at school		
8·00 – 8·30	Cover absent Staff		
8·30 – 8·40	Senior Staff meet (briefing session)		
8·45 – 9·00	Take school assembly		
9·05 – 9·45	Free		
9·45 – 10·20	Teach 2nd Form		
10·20 – 10·40	Break		
10·40 – 11·55	Free		
11·55 – 12·20	Lunch time Supervision		
12·20 – 1·00	Lunch		
1·00 – 2·15	Teach 5th GCSE Class		
2·15 – 2·50	Teach 3rd Form		
2·50 – 3·30	Free		
3·30 – 5·00	Heads of Dept. Curriculum meeting		

Part 2:
Bestwick Park High School 8.00:

When you reach your office you find the following messages in
your in-tray. Use the second column of your time management
sheet to restrucure your day. Can you still accommodate all the
demands on your time?

1

MEMO TO: The Deputy Head   7.30 am
MEMO FROM: J. Briggs, Caretaker

Dear Mrs Perkins,

The 6th Form Common Room is in
a complete mess again.
I think it should be closed
until they learn they can't treat
it as a dump.

Sorry to bother you.
         John Briggs,
                    Caretaker.

2

MEMO TO: Mrs. Perkins

MEMO FROM: Ellen Drives, School Sec.

Mr Dawkins, Chairman of the P.T.A. rang after you left yesterday. He wants to pop in at lunchtime to discuss arrangements for the school fête on Saturday. Is this OK? I said I thought it was, but that you would ring to confirm this in the morning.

Ellen.

3

MEMO TO: Yvonne

MEMO FROM: Ian Brill, Head of Science

Dear Yvonne,

    I am very concerned about what I have heard about the curriculum proposals that we are to discuss tonight. The implications for the Science Department are horrendous.

Can I see you before the meeting takes place?

Ian.

Part 3:

Later developments:

9.30 You talk to Ellen Driver, the secretary, as soon as she arrives and discover that the office is way behind with all its work. Your curriculum paper is not ready.

At break, as you return to your office, you find Sunitti Pattni, Head of Third Year, waiting for you. She is very concerned about Julie Marsh, whom she found crying in the cloakroom during Assembly . . .

> *When I kept asking her what the matter was, she came out with a very garbled story about sexual abuse at her 'uncle's'. I can't tell whether it's true – she's always had a lurid imagination, but we can't just ignore it, can we?*

You certainly can't ignore it, especially as you, as first deputy, are the named teacher ie the contact point for possible sexual abuse.

Your day is certainly not turning out according to plan. It would take superhuman ability or a 36 hour day to fit everything in, so what are you going to do? Use our method of prioritising tasks according to urgency and importance to sort out how you are going to tackle the tasks you now face.

6 Dealing with administration

What does your job entail if you are the Administrative Deputy and your job description includes *The daily running of the school*? Figure 5 illustrates some of the functions your role may include. These responsibilities vary from school to school, but the following are likely to be among them:

Figure 5

1 Dealing with daily cover for absence and room changes

Covering for absent colleagues is a major part of the job of the Administrative Deputy and is never popular with staff. However, it does give you a lot of power because anyone needing cover for whatever reason will have to come and negotiate with you. Whatever system you devise must be clear and be seen to be fair. Having favourites who never appear on the cover sheet, while other staff regularly have to cover particularly difficult classes, will make you very unpopular indeed with the majority of the staff.

You will probably need to start analysing the free periods of all the teaching staff so that you know how many staff are free for each teaching period and how many non-contact periods each person has. There is no perfect system to use, especially as the organisation of teaching day and the amount of absence varies from school to school. Some staff prefer to know that they are most likely to lose Thursday period 3 each week and that Friday period 4 is safe unless there is an epidemic or major crisis, other staff prefer to lose a different period each time. They will want to know that, as far as possible, everyone is losing roughly the same proportion of their free time; that means that you will need to keep a record of who is used each week. The easiest method is to keep a book with staff names down one side and the weeks across the top (see page 90). This is also a useful quick check for you if you are trying to rotate people, as you can easily see how frequently you have used them for a particular period. The most unpopular cover is always last period in the day, particularly if staff who are free are allowed to leave early if they are not needed. So if you want to check that your system is working monitor last period in the day over half a term. If the same member of staff has had to do cover for last period in the day several weeks in succession, there will soon be mutterings against you in the staffroom.

Covering staff who are absent is central to the efficient running of the school. It is important that cover is arranged early enough for staff to see it before they have to go to teach, and if possible before registration. Known absence can be covered in advance so that you are only left to deal with that day's sickness at the last moment. It is essential that cover is organised carefully so that people are not asked to cover when they are not free, sent to the wrong place or used twice – and so that classes are not left without cover. If a member of staff is taken ill during the day and additional cover has to be posted, it is your job to see that the staff who are being used are informed that they are needed. All this may sound obvious, but with the increase of Inset activity the volume of cover can be considerable and it is easy to make mistakes. Always check back before you post the cover notice so that you avoid errors – if you fail to do so you will be regarded as incompetent and lose the respect of the staff.

The same principle applies to organising room changes. You should post known changes well in advance and your notice must be clearly expressed so everybody involved understands what is expected of him or her.

2   Co-ordinating events and functions

The Administrative Deputy usually acts as co-ordinator for some or all of the regular events and functions that occur during each term and which interrupt the normal functioning of the school. You will have to organise some of these events yourself, but for others you will have liaise with and supervise the member of staff who is responsible for the function eg in some schools the Deputy Head organises Parents' Evenings, in others the Year Heads take responsibility but under the overall supervision of the Deputy Head. School photographs, administrative arrangements for concerts and other productions, induction of new pupils, open evenings and speech day or prize giving are the kinds of event you may have to organise. Sports Day arrangements are likely to be dealt with by the Head of PE but he/she should first liaise with you. For all these events you will have to work out the arrangements and communicate them clearly to everyone involved.

3   Dealing with crises

> *Someone has dropped a bottle of noxious fluid and the whole Science block has to be evacuated. The electricity has failed just as afternoon school has begun. Workmen arrive unexpectedly to repair the blinds in several classrooms ...*

These are just a few examples of the crises for which you cannot plan and that disrupt even the best-managed institution. Emergencies can never be left till later but must be dealt with immediately, even if you have to arrange cover for your own class while you see to it. It is important to remain calm. It is your responsibility to decide what is to be done and to communicate this effectively to everyone involved. Few schools have a loudspeaker system so you

It is important to remain calm...

will probably have to use notices and runners. Make sure that
no-one who needs the information is left out; if a class has to
operate in particularly difficult conditions it is usually worth going
to explain personally.

4   Producing the calendar of events

Your responsibilities are likely to include arranging the school's
cycle of meetings and functions. Some schools prefer to fix all
meetings for a certain day of the week, so that, for example, the
staff meeting, Heads of Department, Departmental meetings,
Heads of Year and Year meetings all occur on Tuesdays on a
rotating basis. Other schools prefer to vary the days, eg staff
meeting on Tuesdays, Heads of Department on Wednesdays and
so on ... Examples of the kinds of calendar that you may have to
produce can be found in Case Study 6.1.

What is essential when doing this type of work is that it is
planned out carefully and that you liaise with everyone who is
likely to be affected before you draw up the final list of events.
You may still have to make alterations, but try to change as little

as possible once the list has been published. There is nothing more irritating for staff who are trying to attend all these functions than to find that a parents' evening has been changed at the last minute – even worse, that it was changed some time ago but no-one thought to tell them.

5 Organising/co-ordinating duty rota

One of your tasks as administrative manager may be to co-ordinate the school's staff duty rota. In many schools the Deputy Head has traditionally organised who does the necessary duties but increasingly, as the number of senior management tasks have grown, this has had to be delegated and schools have organised daily duty teams, each with its own leader. You will have to see that these teams work properly and that arrangements are made for sessions when ordinary procedures do not operate, eg the last day of term.

6 Monitoring the school office

The school office processes most of the information that you have to communicate to staff, parents or pupils. The pressure on the office staff and the volume of information with which they have to cope is escalating. Many schools find that a member of the office staff has to act as a full-time receptionist as the telephone or enquirers at the door never stop. It is your responsibility to ensure that they know what the deadlines are and that they meet them. You will probably find that you need at least a weekly session with the secretary to go through the requirements and to check the deadlines and that you have to follow up individual notifications etc. Otherwise some items may get overlooked.

7 Liaison with the caretaker

The caretaker plays a very significant part in how a school presents itself. His/her goodwill is always extremely important, and now more than ever because you are likely to want the number of school lettings to increase in order to expand your income. You have to check that s/he has full information about what is required, with copies of the school calendar and of any special procedures eg parents' evenings which require him/her to put desks and chairs in a particular arrangement in the hall or productions where the stage has to be set up and the hall filled with seats. S/he will want room plans or clear information about the number of chairs etc needed for such events. Another responsibility is to monitor the state of the school and you may need to walk round the school regularly (in some schools as often as once a week), to check the state of the rooms, furniture etc, for damage or graffitti. The caretaker, too, is becoming more of a manager under LMS and this increases the need for good liaison. If s/he complains about the state in which the pupils have left some areas of the school, or the damage caused by a particular letting, let him/her know what action is taken so that s/he can see that you have taken notice of what was said.

Good liaison with the kitchen and other non-teaching staff will also affect the smooth running of the school – do not forget to inform the kitchen if the morning is to be extended and you want the pupils to have dinner later than usual.

8   Internal communications

You have to communicate the arrangements that you have made as clearly as you can. Internally you will usually have space on the main staff noticeboard for urgent or regular notices eg cover arrangements. Some form of news bulletin, weekly or even daily, has become common in schools. If you deal with daily administration, producing it will fall to your lot. If you have to make last-minute changes it is your responsibility to ensure that everyone knows about them. Effective communication with staff is treated fully in Chapter 7, some examples of how you can convey administrative information can be found in Case Study 6.1.

9   External communications

You will probably also be responsible for drafting notifications to parents, about parents' evenings, term dates, end-of-term arrangements, functions etc. For a lot of these (eg parents' evenings) you will be able to develop a standard format so that you need only change the date, or you can adapt similar letters. With practice this should not prove time-consuming for you. Do, however, always remember to check that dates and days of the week are correct and allow plenty of time, usually about three or four weeks, between the letter and the event.

10 Managing examinations

The organisation of examinations varies enormously from school to school. In some schools it falls solely to one person, often a senior teacher, in others, the task can be spread among a number of staff, and divided into internal and external examinations. The external examinations themselves may be divided according to the board or type. If you are the administrative Deputy you will have to liaise with one or more examinations officer(s) and either you or the examinations officer will have to deal with the rooms and invigilation required for the examinations. This can be a time-consuming operation and there are few short cuts. Our advice is that if this is one of your responsibilities – make sure that you allow sufficient time and attention to deal with it all thoroughly and check your arrangements meticulously to make sure that you do a good job. Making a mess of examination arrangements affects a lot of people and could lose you some much-needed goodwill.

Case Study 6.1   *For reflection*
**DEALING WITH ADMINISTRATION AT
BESTWICK PARK HIGH SCHOOL**

Yvonne Perkins is the Deputy Head with responsibility for the daily running of the school. Here are some examples of how she deals with day-to-day administration. How effectively do you think she is carrying out her task?

Example 1: COVER ARRANGEMENTS

NB for multiple cover Mrs Perkins has a different form.

BESTWICK PARK HIGH SCHOOL   COVER SHEET

STAFF. Mr R Willis ...... SUBJECT. Science ...

DAY. Wednesday .... DATE. 13th May .....

FORM. 3W .... ROOM. 5 ....

Staff required for:

(a) Morning registration..) Mrs S. Pattni .....

(b) Afternoon registration.) ....

(c) Duty... ─ ....

If no work has been provided, please see Head

of Department concerned

PERIOD	FORM	ROOM	STAFF REQUIRED
1	4ths	Physics Lab. 1	Mrs Higgs
2			Mr Draper
3			
4	3A I.T.	Computer Lab.	Ms Prince
5	L6 AL	Physics Lab 1.	No cover needed
6	L6 AL		No cover needed
7	2nds	Physics Lab 1.	Mrs Croft
8	2nds	"	Mr Tucker

Please see the Lab. Technician who has Mr Willis' work.

Example 2

Bestwick Park High School

DATE Wednesday 5th March   <u>Daily Bulletin</u>

1.Staff absent or out of school

Mrs Gatlin (pm) Heads' meeting

Mr Draper and Mr Parks - supply for course
= Mrs Frost

Mrs Hills

2.Expeditions, etc

None

3.Meetings or special events

(a) During school

Repairs to Hut 3. Please see room changes list

(b) After school

Heads of Department Meeting 3.30pm
in Room 6

4.Visitors:

Mrs Sibley — T.V.E.I. Co-ordinator to see
Mr Wade

Today's duty team: Mrs Michael's team

Example 3

BESTWICK PARK HIGH SCHOOL - CYCLE OF TUESDAY MEETINGS - AUTUMN TERM

STAFF MEETING	5TH SEPTEMBER
HEADS OF DEPARTMENT MEETING	12TH SEPTEMBER
HEADS OF YEAR MEETING	19TH SEPTEMBER
DEPARTMENT MEETINGS	26TH SEPTEMBER
YEAR MEETINGS	10TH OCTOBER
STAFF MEETING	31ST OCTOBER
HEADS OF DEPARTMENT MEETING	8TH NOVEMBER
HEADS OF YEAR MEETING	21ST NOVEMBER
DEPARTMENT MEETINGS	5TH DECEMBER
YEAR MEETINGS	12TH DECEMBER

Example 4

BESTWICK PARK HIGH SCHOOL

ROOM CHANGES   Repairs to Hut 3

DATE	PERIOD	CLASS	DISPLACED FROM	TO GO TO	STAFF INVOLVED
5th March	P1	3M	Hut 3	Room 1	Mr Briggs
"	P2	5G	Hut 3	Home Econ. Room	Mrs Croft
"	P3-4	4A	Hut 3	Room 5	Miss Prince
"	P5	2B	Hut 3	Hut 6	Miss Southern
"	P7-8	5K	Hut 3	Room 12	Mr McTavish

Example 5

BESTWICK PARK HIGH SCHOOL

SCHOOL INITIATIVES

STAFF RELEASE – MONTHLY RETURN

MAY

NAME OF INITIATIVE	DATE	NAME OF TEACHER RELEASED	NAME OF SUPPLY TEACHER	NUMBER OF PERIODS
Humanities Modular Course development	May 7th	Mrs Michael Mr Blake Mrs Croft	Mrs Feast	4 periods (pm)
Science Dept. Preparation for National Curriculum	May 10th	Mr Tucker Mrs Trevor Mr Jones Mr Willis Ms Custard	Mrs Green Miss Knight	4p am. 4p am.
Nuffield AL Chemistry (course)	May 15th	Mr Tucker	Mrs Green	4p pm.
Performing Arts	May 16th	Ms Prince	Mr Cheadley	6p.
R.E. A.S. level courses	May 19th	Mrs Stringer	Mrs Feast	6p.
Management Foundation Course	May 23rd–24th	Mrs Michael	Mrs Feast	2 full days.

Example 6

Bestwick Park High School staff cover record autumn term

	4/9	11/9	18/9	25/9	2/10	9/10	16/10	30/10	6/11	13/11	20/11	27/11	4/12	11/12	18/12
Mrs S Barnes		F1			m1										
Mr R Blake		W2			Th6										
Mrs F Bruce	Th4			W3											
Mrs E Croft		F7			m3	F7									
Mr C Draper		F8			Th7										
Mr D Farr DH				W8											
Mr F Fairweather		W5			Th2										
Ms P Francis			W2		m4										
Mr P Greenwood		F8													
Mrs J Higgs		W6				F3									
Miss M Hemmings			W7			F7									
Mrs L Hills	Th3			F7											
Mrs M Jardine			F3			Tu3									
Mrs K King			F8			Th7									
Mr G Lamm		F3		F4											
Mr P McKensie	Th5			F3		Th5									
Mr H McTavish			F7		m8										
Miss F Marshall			F4			Tu8									
Mr P Marshall				W3		F8									
Mrs V Michael			F5			Th6									
Mr N North			W1			M6									
Mrs Y Perkins DH							Tu1								
Mr G Perks			Tu8				Th4								
Ms P Prince			Tu7				F4								
Mrs S Pattni				M4			Th8								
Ms V Southern				M1			Tu7								
Mrs J Stringer			Tu4												
Mrs H Trevor		W3		W4											
Mr S Tucker			Tu2		Th5										
Mr M Wade DH			F8												
Mr R Willis			Tu1		Th8										

7 Managing communications

Good communications are what make school management effective. The modern secondary school is a large and complex organisation and there is a lot happening. As a senior manager carrying out a range of tasks, conveying information and convincing an audience are vitally important aspects of your job. Your communications network is likely to be very wide (see Figure 6).

What is the purpose of the communication?

1 To convey information
If the necessary information does not reach the people concerned, or if they cannot understand the arrangements because they are not expressed clearly, then you cannot expect cooperation or that the arrangements will work.

2 To receive information
If you have failed to set up a mechanism whereby you receive information, eg about when rooms are required or are out of use, you will find it very difficult to carry out your administrative tasks.

3 To discuss an issue
You will need to produce discussion papers to air an issue or problem. You will also have to lead meetings devoted to discussing any prospective change to the system.

4 To convince – ie to gain approval or acceptance of a project
As a senior manager you are often responsible for formulating or implementing change. You will need to gain support or acceptance from a variety of groups, eg staff, pupils, parents, for the project.

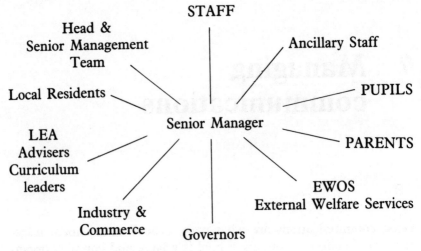

Figure 6   *Your communications network*

Successful communication can be formal or informal, oral or written. What is important is that it is appropriate for the purpose and that it is effective.

Two tests for an effective communications system are:

1 Can everyone find out everything that they need to know easily, ie at the least cost in terms of time and effort?
2 Does everyone feel part of a system which is sensitive to his/her needs?

Internal communications

No-one seems to tell us what anyone else is doing. I know that there are lots of committees and working parties, but I am not involved in most of them, and I really do not know what is happening in the school. If there is a feedback procedure, it seems to have passed me by . . .

(Biology teacher)

We keep them informed as far as we can, but the goal posts seem to change daily at the moment, and sometimes we have progressed two or three more stages before there is an opportunity to tell the staff about the latest developments and they think that we are trying to conceal things from them . . .

(Deputy Head)

They just do not seem to want to listen. I tell them everything that I can, but they really do not want to hear, because it means that they have to change the way that they work. They say, 'What has this got to do with us? These things are senior management responsibilities.' They are trying to bury their heads in the sand . . .

(Head)

The quotations above indicate one of the problems faced by senior managers in a school today – that of communicating with staff – and give three perceptions of the problem. A school is a hive of activity and it is very easy for an individual member of staff to miss out on what is going on. If this continues for any length of time it can lead to a situation where resentment builds up as people begin to feel left out, and staff become critical of the senior management team for its failure to consult or communicate. An ability not only to communicate information but also to obtain a favourable response has become a necessity for a senior manager. Here are some ideas for communicating with staff.

1 Hold a regular briefing session

A briefing session is a short staff meeting for the purpose of giving information. There are two ways of organising this kind of session – daily or weekly. If it is regular it does not have to be long; it needs only to be five or at the most ten minutes. If it is weekly rather than daily then you will probably want ten to 15 minutes. Most of the information will be given by the Head or a member of the senior management team, but there is also the opportunity for staff to inform other staff of particular activities in their section of the school or to ask for help. The briefing session, however, has another use besides letting the staff know what is going on in the school, it is informal contact time between the Head and the staff. Often it is difficult for a member of staff to get to see the Head, particularly about a minor matter where it seems silly to book an appointment. A senior management team which has its finger on the pulse of the school will pick up 'vibes' from the mood of the meeting and will linger in the staff room for a few minutes at the end of the briefing to give the staff an opportunity to talk to them.

2   Produce a daily information sheet

This kind of sheet (see page 97) is not intended for major issues. It is simply to inform staff of the events of the day and serves as a reminder of what is going on. It takes about five minutes to produce and is usually the job of whoever deals with daily administration/cover. It will tell you such things as who is away; if a form is going on an expedition, so that you will know that you are not teaching them; if there are any visitors or activities so that strangers can be identified, welcomed and directed appropriately; and if particular rooms are not available for use that day.

3   Produce a regular news bulletin for staff

A news bulletin needs to be issued weekly. Much of it will be taken up with administrative notices, as it will inform staff of the events of that particular week, especially as the termly calendar of events is likely to need to be modified as the term proceeds, but it will also include reports from working parties or committees (see Case Study 7.3). The bulletin is a good vehicle to convey an update on the progress of a committee, in a short form.

4   Produce a working paper

A working paper can either be a discussion document aimed at summing up the arguments about a current issue or a briefing document intended to provide more information than you can convey orally at a meeting. As a senior manager you will need to learn to produce this kind of paper so that it does not take you much time to draft, yet makes its points clearly and effectively. (Some examples of working papers appear in other chapters of this book eg Staff Development.)

5   Organise working party reports

If a working party wants to convey a lot of information, it is better to do so through a working paper devoted to that particular topic. If you are in charge of communications, it would be your task to agree with the chairperson of the working group, what the purpose and format of that paper should be. Staff need to be informed, but will not want to be swamped with information or paper. One to two sides of A4 at the most will serve the purpose but it needs to be used effectively.

6 Devote a whole staff meeting to one issue

An effective use of a full staff meeting can be to devote it to an awareness raising session. The introduction of LMS is an obvious example where the senior management team have needed to do a 'teach-in' with the staff to prepare them for major changes in how the school would be run.

Similarly a staff meeting can be used to sound out staff views on an issue and to discuss it through with them.

7 Set up a consultative committee

Feedback from the staff helps the senior management team to know how the staff have reacted to the information that they have received. Picking up vibes from the staffroom can be a very hit or miss method. Some schools have set up a small consultative committee to act as a sounding board and to make representations on behalf of the staff if there are issues about which staff are worried or concerned. Make sure that this committee is kept separate from any social committee that the staff may have as its purpose is quite different.

Some pointers to effective communications
- Know what you are trying to achieve. Be clear about the purpose of a document or meeting.
- Do not try to do too many things at once, thus obscuring the issue.
- Make sure everyone understands the aim of a meeting – ie whether it is to be a discussion or an information session. Otherwise people may feel that the discussion was muffled, whereas the purpose was to inform, with a separate meeting scheduled for discussing the issue.
- Put out a discussion or information paper before the

> meeting. This gives people time to consider the issues –
> essential if there is to be a vote.
> - Make sure you include the personal element – people
>   always want to know how a change will affect them and
>   what they are expected to do.
> - Think about how you put things over. Using the appro-
>   priate form of communication needs as much thought as
>   what you want to say.

Case Study 7.1   *For discussion*
COMMUNICATING WITH STAFF

Here are three examples of senior managers communicating with
staff: Do they communicate information effectively and, more
important, what kind of a response will they provoke?

1

```
Dear Mrs Feast,

            Unfortunately we shall have to cut your teaching
time next year to about half the amount you have been working
this year as under LMS our budget is substantially reduced.

            Yours sincerely,

            Yvonne Perkins, Curriculum Deputy.
```

2

```
I told you quite clearly that I wanted the draft proposal

by today at the latest.  Now we shall probably lose our

chance of securing funding...
```

The Inset Co-ordinator is furious with the Head of Modern
Languages, who yet again has failed to meet a deadline. The
confrontation takes place in the staffroom ...

3

```
I've fixed a meeting of the curriculum committee for Tuesday -
OK?
```

Mrs Perkins to Mrs Michael, Head of Humanities, as they pass in the corridor.

Case Study 7.2   *Exemplar*
A NEWS BULLETIN

BESTWICK PARK HIGH SCHOOL   10 May
                    STAFF NEWS BULLETIN

Profiling Working Party Report
We are pleased to be able to report that we now have a draft
profile ready to trial with the Fourth Year after half term.
In the meantime it is available for you to see. They were
put into pigeon holes on Monday morning so everyone should
have received a personal copy. If for some reason you did
not receive a copy please ask me (J.W.) for one. We should
be grateful for your comments (in writing please). It is
important that they reach me by May 20th if modifications
are to be made.
                    Joanne Ward, Working Party Chair

Staff Committee announcements
The date of the end of term party has been fixed for
Thursday July 23rd - so please put the date into your diary.
The venue will be the school hall - outside if the weather
permits. We have booked the same caterer as last year, but
need to know whether you want us to book a band before we
can tell you what the price will be. We hope that the
function will be even better than last year.
                    Cherry Chase, Chair Staff Committee

Expeditions this week
Tues 11th Geography Field Trip - whole second year to St
Albans. Please see arrangements sheet for staff involved.
Staff who normally teach second years may find that they
have been used to cover the classes of teachers involved in
the trip.
Friday 14th Art Dept. A/L pupils with Miss Brush to
exhibition at the Royal Academy.

Staff out
Mrs Stringer - RE day course Comparative Religion, Weds
12th. Mrs Gatlin - out of school at Heads' meetings on
Monday afternoon and all day Thursday.

Inset
Humanities pilot schools meeting here - Thurs 13th from
1.30pm. Continues after school. Location: History Room (Room
12). Faculty members involved: Mrs Michael and Mrs Draper
(supply teacher Mrs Fray will cover). Please direct any
visitors who look like lost Humanitarians towards the
History Room!

Visitors
Mr Rowse - our link Adviser. Weds am to see Miss Prince
(probationer). Mrs Grant - Chairman of Governors to see the
Head, Weds pm.

Governors' meeting
Thurs 13th, 7.30pm in the Library.

The most important point about a staff news bulletin such as that
issued at Bestwick Park is that it should tell you everything you
need to know. Apply this acid test to information bulletins issued
in your school.

Drafting documents

Now that you are a senior manager a significant proportion of your
time will be spent in drafting written communications. The kinds
of document you may have to produce could include:

- a working paper – a discussion paper to air an issue
- a briefing sheet – giving information about an event or topic
- a report – eg of the activities of a working party
- a statement of intent – eg a proposal or bid for funding
- a development plan – covering one, three or even five years
- an evaluation – eg of the progress of an initiative

Some tips for drafting a document
- Plan it out first, so that you know what you want to say
  and how you are going to say it.
- It should be easy to read. Complicated ideas can be
  expressed simply and clearly.
- Keep it as short as possible.
- Each section should be clearly headed, so that the reader
  can follow the organisation of the document.
- Summarise points at the end of each section as this makes
  a difficult paper easier to understand.
- Avoid jargon where possible.
- Check that it includes all the information that you want
  to convey.

Case Study 7.3
A REPORT   *Examplar*

REPORT OF THE CURRICULUM COMMITTEE

The membership of this committee comprised: Mr M Wade,
Mrs M Jardine, Mr S Tucker, Mrs K King, Miss M Hemmings,
Miss F Marshall, Mr R Willis. Chair: Mrs Y Perkins

The committee met three times in the Autumn Term - Sept
19th, Oct 21st and Nov 15th.

Its terms of reference were to review the curriculum
provision for our 16 - 19 pupils in the light of the NCC
report to the Secretary of State for Education, and
suggest what approaches should be taken.

Its recommendations are as follows:

1 Review of the CPVE Course by the CPVE Team, to check i)
that the necessary skills are being accessed; ii) that
sufficient breadth and balance are being provided. A
half-day INSET session should be provided out of the
school's Inset budget for the team to carry out this
work.

2 Map A and A/S courses to discover which skills each
accessed. To be carried out in the Spring Term by Kate
King in her TVEI release time.

3 A sub-committee should be established to identify the
most cost-effective ways of changing our current General
Studies courses to meet the new demands. Spring Term,
Margaret Jardine to Chair.

4 Expansion of tutorial provision through the
introduction of a weekly tutor period. Mrs Perkins to
check timetable implications.

5 Mrs Jardine and Miss Hemmings to consult Advisory
Teacher for profiles about creating a Record of
Achievement that would fit both CPVE and A level
students.

6 Mrs Jardine, as Head of Sixth, to produce a three-year
development paper for 16 - 19, on the basis of this
committee's suggestions and the mapping exercises.
Summer Term.

                    A D Perkins, 21st November

This report tells you who was on the committee, how often it met,
its terms of reference, what its recommendations were and who
will be carrying out the work. Note that it does not need to be
long or chatty.

Case Study 7.4   *For reflection*
DRAFTING A DISCUSSION PAPER

REWARDS AND SANCTIONS - DISCUSSION PAPER

During the last academic session the School Council
discussed rewards and sanctions. From this discussion it
emerged that it was felt that the existing system was not
being used and needed to be reviewed and opinion among
girls, parents and staff suggested that there would be
support for an enhanced system of rewards as well as a
clearer system of sanctions. There was also some support for
the view that at present in the school sport is rewarded
more than academic achievement and that this should be
balanced by an increase in the number of other rewards
given.

REWARDS
Although it was recognised that a high standard of work and
achievement brings its own rewards, it was felt that some
tangible rewards should be given. After taking soundings the
Year Tutors discussed the matter at some length and have
devised the following suggested scheme:

1 Commendations
Commendations already exist in the school, but are not
widely used by staff at present. It was felt, however, that
the use of commendations should be extended and that they
should become the school's formal method of rewarding good
work, service or personal achievement. It was felt that a
commendation form should be used as this gave the
commendation more status than signing the commendation book.
The procedure would work as follows: when a commendation is
given to a pupil, the teacher should fill in the
commendation form, sign it and give it to the pupil who
should take it to the Year Tutor. This will give the Year
Tutor the opportunity to encourage good work and effort. The
Year Tutor will then hand the slip to the Form Tutor so that
the commendation can be recorded in order to contribute to
the pupil's record of achievement.

2 Prizes
Although there were some reservations, the majority of staff
favoured the introduction of prizes. It was not felt,
however, that these should necessarily all be money
prizes/book tokens, nor was it felt that there should be a
large number of prizes as this defeated the purpose of
giving them at all. It is therefore proposed that there
should be one prize per year group: given for service to the
school and that the Parents' Association should be
approached to donate these prizes.
  The school has been approached recently and on a number of
occasions in the past by Computers International, who wish
to donate a prize or prizes to the school. It was felt that
the offer should be accepted and it would be appropriate to
commemorate our past Chairman of Governors, L M Smith, by
establishing an L M Smith Memorial Prize, to be given for
academic excellence. (The amount may be sufficient to reward
more than one pupil.)

It was felt that any other 'prizes' should take the form of certificates of merit, to be awarded annually and presented at Year Assemblies. Merit was to encompass achievement, effort and behaviour and recipients were to be chosen by the Year Tutor in consultation with form staff.

3 Trophies
It was felt desirable to incorporate the award of trophies into the system, especially in view of the number of trophies at present awarded for sport. The school already has a number of trophies which are not being used. Awarding a cup for the most commendations in each year group seemed an appropriate way to encourage the extension of the system of commendations and it was decided to include the sixth form in this arrangement. Some thought was given to other areas where trophies could be awarded and suggestions here included: an English oral cup; a debating cup; a modern languages oral cup(s).

SANCTIONS
It was felt that at present the school's system of sanctions was not operating effectively and that some restructuring was needed. The following system was therefore suggested:

1 Cautions
A caution would be given for such things as bad behaviour, homework not being done/given in etc. When a caution is given to a pupil, the teacher concerned should fill in the caution slip. (This time it is not countersigned by the pupil.) Caution slips should be given to the Year Tutor, who will see the pupil. The slip will then be given to the Form Tutor who will place it on the pupil's file.

2 Detentions
Three cautions will result in a detention, as will a particularly serious offence. This system will be administered by the Year Tutors and parents will need to be given at least 48 hours notice if a pupil is to be detained.

3 Weekly report
It was felt that weekly report served a different function from detention and that it should be used (sparingly) for persistent misconduct, lateness or homework not completed, where we felt the need to monitor or support a pupil. The subject teacher will be asked to sign the report at the end of each week. A list of pupils on weekly report will be posted in the staffroom so that staff will know which pupils are on report at any time.

4 Suspension
Suspension is only used for very severe offences. The rules governing suspension are set out in the Education Act (2) 1986. Only the Head Teacher can suspend a pupil and the LEA and the governors have to be involved.

For reflection
1 How far does this document fulfil the criteria for drafting a good discussion paper? (The process of producing this paper is described in Chapter 7 Managing the Pastoral System)

2   Examples of development plans and other documents may be found throughout the book.

Making a presentation

The Head asked me to talk to a parents' meeting about the proposed change from separate History and Geography courses to an Integrated Humanities course in the junior section of the school. I had never addressed a really large audience before and no-one gave me any advice about how to prepare properly. I had a list of points that I wanted to make and some OHPs that I could use, but on the night I was much more nervous than I expected. I was largely inaudible, apparently my voice drops towards the end of sentence, and in my nervousness, I did not realise that I was standing in front of my OHPs so that no-one could see them and this irritated the audience. When the Head asked for questions there were some complicated technical questions. I gave detailed answers which clearly bored many of the audience and I had difficulty finding the information because my notes had got out of order. There were also quite a lot of hostile questions or comments disguised as questions. One parent became extremely aggressive about what he called the lack of rigour of the new course and just wouldn't let up; in the end the Head had to rescue me.

(Vivienne Michael, Head of the Humanities Faculty
at Bestwick Park describing a recent experience)

Vivienne had clearly failed to impress the audience of parents that she addressed, and this did not augur well for the changes to the curriculum that she wanted to introduce.

As a senior manager you will have to cope with making a presentation. You may have to present information about a new initiative or a current issue to a variety of possible audiences, who may include: a section of the staff, a full staff meeting; a governors' meeting, the PTA, or an audience of parents. Vivienne's experience of having to explain and convince parents about a proposed change to the curriculum is a typical example. Taking whole school or a year assembly is another form of making a presentation. The length of the presentation will also vary from a short ten minute input to a staff meeting to an address to a hall full of parents, that could last up to an hour or more.

Making a presentation is thus becoming an regular part of the work of a senior manager in a school. Most of us are not born speech makers, but as with other management skills, we can improve our performance through good preparation and practice. The following section is designed to help you avoid the kind of mistakes that Vivienne Michael made and perform effectively when you have to make a presentation.

Methods of making a presentation?

There are five main methods of making a presentation:

1   *Write out the presentation and read it*
This is probably the safest method, but it is generally considered to be the worst. This is because we do not speak as we write. If we use this method we lose directness and immediacy; we do not sound natural. We also lose the advantage of eye contact with the audience, which we may need to help us get a favourable response if the content of the presentation is controversial. This method however, gives you more security than any of the others and particularly when you are new in post and unsure of yourself this may be your best bet, so that you can be sure that the ideas come out accurately and in the right order and that you use the best phrases to describe them. Later on you may come to prefer a method which gives you more flexibility.

2   *Write out the presentation and memorise it*
This is the least flexible method. The talk has to be delivered as it was committed to memory, this will make it sound very stilted and if there are interruptions, it will be very difficult for you to pick up the thread again.

3   *Prepare the ideas, but decide the exact wording at the time of the presentation*
This is the favoured method of most good speakers. It is more natural and flexible than the first two methods, allows for eye contact and is generally more convincing. If you want to use this method, construct an outline plan of what you want to say on a piece of paper or series of cards. It is best to write only simple

headings, catchwords or prompts to your memory as complicated sentences can distract from your flow.

4   *A mixture – memorise the more complicated parts,*
     extemporise the rest
This does not tend to be effective as there is no continuity of approach.

5   *An impromptu speech – think on your feet*
Here you have no prepared text and will need to think very fast on your feet. Usually this only occurs when you are called upon unexpectedly. Then you have to use whatever knowledge and skill is available to you at that moment!

A technique for impromptu speeches
Think of five fingers of a hand. The thumb is the introduction; the forefinger introduces an idea; the middle finger puts the antithesis; the fourth finger is the synthesis and the little finger is the conclusion – 'Telling them what I've told them'.

Preparing a presentation

Preparing your presentation well gets you off to a good start. It should also help build up your confidence. Some points to think about when preparing a presentation are:

1   *Establish your objectives*   Work out what you want to achieve with the presentation.
2   *Analyse your audience*   Your presentation should be appropriate for your audience. Analysing the audience will help you determine:
    • your general style and approach
    • the level of your presentation
    • how much technical language/jargon to include
    • how much supporting material to use, eg statistics, visual aids . . .
3   *Make a preliminary plan*   Sort out your material into essential and additional information.
4   *Organise your material clearly* into three sections:

- the Opening, which captures the audience's attention and introduces your purpose and main ideas. The opening should take no more than 5% of the total time.
- the Main Section, which develops and explains your ideas.
- the Conclusion, which rounds off the presentation, ending on a high note. Summaries are often a useful and systematic way of concluding.

When you organise your material, try to begin with opinions with which the audience will agree. This gives the audience confidence in you so that they are willing to listen to the rest of what you have to say. Include some anecdotes, humour, illustrations etc, to capture attention and provide variety. But be careful that these items do not distract the audience from the main issue. Beware of only including one side of the argument, particularly where the issue is controversial. A heavily-biased presentation is usually received badly, so show that you are aware of, and have considered, opposing arguments.

5 *Prepare your visual aids* These need to be clear and legible, otherwise they will irritate the audience.

6 *Be realistic* about how much material you can expect to cover in the time available.

7 *Keep it short* Audience research indicates that attention begins to waver after 15 minutes and reaches saturation after 30 minutes. Discard most of the non-essential material. You do not want to lose the audience's attention. Limit yourself to four or five main points – it is harder for a listener to absorb information than it is for a reader. A short presentation, with plenty of time for questions, is an effective way of maintaining interest.

Introducing your ideas – Some techniques
- Use a direct statement – *I am going to talk about . . .*
- Use an indirect statement – *You may be wondering why I asked you all to come.*
- Use an example – *Last week the following incident occurred . . .*
- Use a quotation – *X once said . . .*
- Use statistics – *The cost of a main grade member of staff is . . .*
- Use humour – a funny story used as an icebreaker.

A speaker's checklist

Before you begin, run through the following mental checklist:

1   Do you sound and look natural and relaxed?
2   Are you standing comfortably? (Try standing with feet slightly apart and the weight of the body on the balls of the feet. Your arms are best hanging easily at your side or behind you. Only sit down if the audience is very small.)
3   Do you fiddle constantly with your notes or the chalk?
4   Can you smile at your audience and get some of them to smile back?
5   Have you practised and rehearsed your speech? A runthrough will show you where you may have difficulties.
6   Do you speak slowly enough for people to follow what you say? Can you vary the pace appropriately?
7   Are you audible? Is the pitch varied? Is there light and shade? Are the consonants clearly sounded, especially the end ones? Is the overall effect pleasant?
8   Have you got the time checkpoints marked in your notes or do you have to rush to cover everything in time?
9   Are your signposts clear to the audience? (They should mark the end of one section and beginning of another.)
10   Do you remember to summarise leads or reinforce points at the end of a section of the presentation?
11   How often do you say 'um' or 'er' or keep clearing your throat?
12   Are your gestures effective devices to emphasise important points or do they distract or irritate the audience?
13   Can you move your eyes across (traverse) your audience while you speak?

To use this checklist effectively ask a colleague to observe one of your presentations and offer feedback – then act on it!

Answering questions

Dealing with questions from the floor can be more nerve-racking than making a speech, because it is difficult to anticipate precisely what will be asked. You have to convince the audience that you are sufficiently knowledgeable about the subject under discussion and that you can think on your feet. Yet it is an excellent way of making contact with an audience. It gives them a chance to participate; it indicates the level of comprehension and it gives you feedback.

Handling questions
- Make it clear to the audience when you will deal with the questions.
- Repeat the question so that everyone knows what it is.
- Make the questioner clarify the question if you do not understand it.
- Do not rush into an answer – take a few moments to analyse the question and work out your answer.
- Do not allow a single questioner to dominate.
- Avoid being aggressive, personal or sarcastic.
- Be clear what is your personal view and what is school policy.
- Do not be drawn into long wrangles with any of the questioners.
- Move your eyes across the audience when you speak.
- Don't ramble on. Keep your answers short and to the point.

Some situations

1 You are Derek Farr, Pastoral Deputy at Bestwick Park High School. You have to make a presentation to the staff about your proposals for restructuring the school's pastoral system. How would you set about it?
2 You are Simon Tucker, Head of the Science Faculty. Mrs Gatlin, the Head, has asked you to address an audience of Third Form parents about the planned introduction of Balanced Science into the Fourth Form curriculum next September.
   How do you set about it?

8 Managing curriculum development

One of the most important roles that a senior manager may have is to be the school's Curriculum Manager. In the past this would have simply meant that you were the school's timetabler, interpreting a curriculum that changed little from year to year. Now all that has changed, if you are the Curriculum Co-ordinator or the Deputy Head Curriculum, you may not do the timetable at all, especially now that schools are becoming computerised. You are pre-eminently a manager, whose task it is to create a curriculum that accommodates external demands and current legislation and also satisfies internal pressures and much of your time will be concerned with development.

Your role as a Curriculum Manager may take various forms:

1   You may be the *catalyst* for development – the person whose analysis of the existing timetable spurs him/her to realisation that it is no longer relevant and that you have got to do away with the option system immediately. Nowadays it is much more likely, however, that the catalyst will be external – the DES; the LEA; TVEI or some similar agency, and that your role will be to react positively to these external demands.

2   It is very tempting for the Curriculum Manager, especially if s/he is new in post, to become the *solution giver*, the person who is sure that s/he has all the answers to how to bring the fourth form curriculum into line with National Curriculum requirements. Even if you have got it right, you would be well advised to remember that you will have to convince all those likely to be affected by the innovations that it is in their

interest to support your plans, or they won't get beyond the drawing board.

3 A good curriculum manager is a *process helper* – a facilitator who has learned to work through other people, helping them with the process of problem solving and innovating. Leading from behind, supporting and facilitating rather than directing is hard work, but development is much more likely to be effective if it is owned by those involved. This kind of curriculum manager has learnt how and when to offer suggestions, and when to let a team run with an initiative.

In this chapter we shall use the example of developing Technology in a girls' comprehensive school. It is typical of the kind of curriculum development which is currently occurring in our schools. It is an externally-imposed change, a part of the local TVEI initiative and thus illustrates the extent to which external factors have now become the driving force for change. It is one of a number of other initiatives which the school will have to develop over the next two or three years. The first task for the curriculum manager will be to work out where this development comes in the school's own priorities, because this will affect how much time and support this particular initiative will receive.

What does managing this kind of curriculum development involve?

If you are the school's Curriculum Manager you will find that there are two aspects to your task. First, it will involve you in a planning exercise as you endeavour to provide a structure or framework for the development. This will necessitate your constructing a *development programme* for the initiative that clarifies your objectives and deals with the timetable of development. (You will find a section on how to draft a development plan later in this chapter.) Second, this task centres on the management of people. You will have to create a team of people to carry out the development. You will need to motivate, enthuse and support this team, not just at the onset of development, but consistently through all its stages. It will involve you in regular sessions with the team leader to monitor progress and to check what is needed. The kind of support you may have to give will vary. It may include providing ideas and suggestions from time to time; it may mean providing resources; it may involve working with the group to find answers to problems, or it could mean getting the Inset Co-ordinator to allocate some supply time through the Inset budget so that the team can have adequate time to modify the course.

You will also have to reconcile the staff as a whole to the fact that yet another major development is to take place. The introduction of Technology is an externally-imposed change – the driving forces are TVEI and the National Curriculum. But there are also internal pressures eg pupil pressure for curriculum opportunity, which push toward this change. A number of people, however, will see it as a threat, some through 'dynamic conservatism' (the desire to continue with the familiar) – there will be staff, parents and governors who will see no need for the introduction of a new subject; others will feel threatened because the new subject constitutes a rival to their own subject for curriculum time or demands expertise that they do not have. Here you will need all your skill as a manager to win support for the development.

Factors influencing curriculum development

Figure 7 illustrates some of the factors you will have to deal with in managing curriculum development.

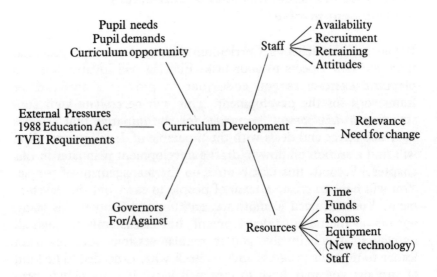

Figure 7

Case Study 8.1   *For reflection*
INTRODUCING TECHONOLOGY

Technology at Eastmount School

Eastmount School was a well-established traditional girls' school. It was about to enter TVEI(E) and had to satisfy the Training Agency that it could deliver Technology within the five year scheme. This was a problem for the school; in common with many other girls' schools, Woodwork, Metalwork and CDT had never formed part of its curriculum, so it had no technology facilities. For Marion Parsons, the TVEI Co-ordinator, the problem was not just the introduction of a new curriculum subject, which needed timetable space and thus threatened other curriculum subjects, but also that Technology was an entirely new subject and it was not at all clear what the curriculum content should be or how it should be delivered. This made the introduction of Technology more difficult than any of the other changes that the school was having to manage.

The school was receiving an increasing number of papers about Technology. Each seemed to have its own definition of the subject. Marion found this both confusing and comforting, confusing as there was no clear guidance, comforting because it appeared that no-one else understood Technology either. Attempting to decipher this plethora of paper brought her to the conclusion that what the school clearly needed was development time and a curriculum development team to deal with it. The introduction of Technology would have to form a five year programme; with little guidance available and neither the facilities nor the subject expertise, they would not be able to progress at a fast rate. In the early stages of the Autumn Term Marion's pessimistic expectation was that although Eastmount school would enter TVEI in the following September, it would not be able to offer Technology to its pupils in year one of the programme.

The TVEI funding arrangements made it possible to offer .1 staffing release for a teacher to co-ordinate Technology. The DES definition at that time said that 'Technology while being a practical and problem solving activity, always has its basis in Science and Mathematics'. Kate King, Head of Physics had already come forward to say that she was interested in developing Technology.

Marion felt it very important that in an area where many staff were unsure or felt threatened, she should build upon enthusiasm. She therefore nominated Kate as the school's Technology Manager. Although a lot was being written about Technology at that time, Marion and Kate soon realised that they would have to find their own solution to the problem of introducing Technology, because it was in such an early stage of development that there was no real fount of outside expertise on which to draw. Their first task was to find the best definition of Technology for the school to adopt. After a lot of thought, they decided that the definition that most suited the school's needs was that used by Berskhire: 'Technology within the curriculum is the purposeful use of inventive thinking and creative activity leading to the production of an artifact or system which best satisfies a perceived need'.

Kate then devised a rough scheme for a skills-based modular course containing elements of graphicacy, electronics and information technology, which could provide an introduction to Technology for the Third Form. But they needed to find curriculum time for it and it was important that Technology should not be introduced at the expense of Arts subjects such as Classics as this would only provoke hostility. Kate was already negotiating with the Head of Information Technology as IT was to form part of the course; these discussions led to the suggestion that the Introduction to Technology course should replace the existing IT course in the Third Form as this had originally been introduced to give pupils hands on experience of computers, which they now gained in the primary school. If the IT course had to be rethought anyway, it made sense to use it as the vehicle for Technology.

Once they had a timetable slot, the course content needed planning, so Marion and Kate set up a task group. They had considered setting up a general working party to develop Technology, but decided that it made better sense to set up a separate task group for each course that needed to be developed. The Third Form Team were given the brief to work out the content of each module; its resource requirements and their own Inset needs. Kate and other members of the team also decided to make some visits to schools in a neighbouring authority where Technology already figured on the curriculum as this would give them ideas about what resources would be needed and because it seemed to them that it would be helpful to see some courses that were already in operation. The visits failed to provide any examples of good practice, but actually increased the team's confidence because they began to appreciate that other schools were not more advanced than Eastmount. This planning work was time-consuming for the staff involved, who gave up some lunch hours and after-school time for meetings, but their morale was boosted by a two very productive half-day working sessions, funded by the school's Inset (LEATGS) budget. By the end of the Spring Term, Marion and Kate could tell the Deputy Head, who was respon-sible for drawing up the timetable, that they could introduce the new course in the following September.

Although this was far better than she had dared to hope only a term earlier, Marion still had the problem that TVEI dealt with pupils aged 14+ and that she and Kate had devised a course for the Third Form. Now they needed to give thought to the Fourth Form curriculum. Here the most appropriate vehicle seemed to be some existing General Studies lessons. These tended to be timetable fillers for both girls and staff and were popular with neither side. It seemed to Marion that whatever happened about Technology these courses needed restructuring, so early in Summer Term she called a meeting of the staff who were being timetabled to run Fourth Year general courses the following year with the agenda of exploring how far they could work together. The departments concerned were Home Economics, IT, Art, Economics and PE. In the meeting each member of staff de-scribed the course that they were likely to offer. As they talked the overlap between courses began to emerge and they began to consider an assignment-based course to which each of their sub-jects could contribute. Eventually George Gemm, the Economics teacher, suggested, 'Why not make my Economic Awareness course into a Mini-enterprise? You could make a product in Home Economics, design the packaging or display in Art, do market research and advertising in IT and run the companies through my Economic Awareness course.'

Marion was delighted. Her five year TVEI plan for the school had included putting some mini-enterprise work into the Fourth Year, but she had been unclear about how to approach this and had doubted that she could do it in the first year of the scheme for more than a small number of pupils. This scheme seemed to offer distinct possibilities and an additional plus point was that all the documents agreed that economic awareness was itself an important element of Technology. The group liked the idea of running a mini-enterprise, but were unsure whether they could do all the course planning in time to implement the scheme in September. It would need a lot of work. They went away to think about it. Several more meetings were held over the next few weeks. They decided to run a modular mini-enterprise from September, but to treat the year as an experimental year because it was so difficult for them to know how they themselves would cope or how the girls would react. In spite of all the hard work, the staff were excited by the challenge, a strong team identity began to emerge as they planned the course, worked out the programme of each module, how and when they had to link together, what their resourcing needs would be, and what problems they would be likely to face. Marion went to all their meetings at the beginning of the planning cycle, but later attended only when they said they needed her. She was extremely impressed with the speed at which they worked and was anxious not to intrude too much. The one stumbling block at this stage was that they could not work out how to include the Physical Education element into the mini-enterprise and therefore decided that for the first year, because of the shortness of planning time, the Fitness Course would have to run alongside the mini-enterprise, but that a planning priority for the team during the next year would be to work out how to integrate it. In the meantime the PE teacher would remain a member of the planning group and participate in all the team Inset.

The resource needs of the two new courses would be met from the school's TVEI budget, but Marion was very aware that projects of this sort created 'haves and have-nots' and that the very excitement of the mini-enterprise team had caused some resentment in more conservative quarters. She discussed this problem with the Head, Miss Hardcastle. They decided that some TVEI funds should go to benefit all staff, not just those involved in delivering TVEI and that they would therefore buy some video equipment that would be popular and used by most subject areas. They thought it important, however, to make it clear to staff that by funding some courses from TVEI, it made it possible to give other non-TVEI courses more money from the school's capitation than they might otherwise have got, so that simply realised that they were *all* gainers from TVEI. They decided that this issue should be discussed at a staff meeting. They also thought that some awareness-raising for the whole staff, both about TVEI and about Technology, would provide the staff with information and also give them an opportunity to air any hostility they might feel, so they invited the TVEI Technology Curriculum Co-ordinator to lead a half-day Inset session for all staff. Although some hostility might remain, this was probably as much as they could do to address the problem; they would have to leave the rest to time and aim to involve an increasing number of teachers in their TVEI programme over the next four years.

By September when Eastmount School entered TVEI Marion had succeeded in introducing two technological courses into the curriculum. This was far more than she could have anticipated a year previously and she and the Head were extremely pleased at the progress that had been made. It was however not the end of development for the school, rather it proved to be the first stage in an ongoing process. It took a year to work out how to integrate the Fitness Course into the Mini-enterprise and longer to work in the school's work experience programme; there were radical changes in the definition and content of Technology to which the school had to adapt and which placed Technology firmly under the aegis of the practical subjects rather than that of Science and Mathematics as had been thought at the start; staff changes affected the structure of the teams, but the flexible approach that Marion had established of overall co-ordination by the TVEI. Co-ordinator and the Technology Manager and the use of task groups to deal with specific problems proved an appropriate mechanism for dealing with the kind of development required for Technology where the goalposts kept changing. Moreover finding that it could cope successfully with change at a rapid pace gave the school confidence to deal with problems as they arose. What they had learnt from the first year of TVEI was that they could successfully develop a new subject from scratch with little guidance or support from any outside agencies.

The case study of the introduction of Technology into East-mount School illustrates a number of points about successful curriculum development:

1 *You may not be provided with a complete picture of the problem, yet you will be expected to offer appropriate solutions*

Marion was presented with a problem in which the nature of the task was not at all clear. She had to think in terms of developing towards a solution, not of finding one immediately. Later she found she could move at a faster rate than she had initially anticipated. Analyse the problem as far as you can, but be prepared to rethink it as and when necessary, particularly in a case where 'the goal posts keep moving'.

2 *You will probably have to draw up a development plan over three or five years*

Marion was planning the TVEI development as a five-year programme. The introduction of Technology was one item in that programme, with its own development cycle. She had to work out the probable timescale and decide priorities. (Advice on how to construct a development plan can be found in later in this Chapter.)

3 *Try to break down a complex task into its component parts or at least more concrete sections*

Marion set up a separate task group to develop each course. This meant that each group could concentrate on one section of the problem. It still entailed a great deal of hard work but the task became more manageable.

4 *Good preparation is essential to successful development*

Marion built planning time into the development programme, including staff Inset sessions and visits to other schools. The cycle of planning meetings was central to the whole development. Preparation needs to be thorough, but that does not mean that progress has to be slow. If a team works well together it can cover a lot of ground in a short time. Where they could not solve a problem immediately, eg with the Fitness Course, they created an appropriate timetable for that part of the development.

5 *Do not forget that curriculum development involves people management as well as task management*

A lot of team building went into the curriculum development. Marion set up her teams and then encouraged them to run with their idea. She made it quite clear that her support was available whenever they needed it, but that she did not wish either to direct or to intrude. Educationalists always stress the importance of ownership to successful curriculum development. This really does mean that the people delivering the course must be its main planners, otherwise they will be less willing to take risks or will blame you if things get difficult.

6 *Building on enthusiasm is often the best way to get started*

Imposing a scheme from the top to be delivered by a reluctant team is rarely successful. Marion was fortunate that she was able to find an interested member of staff with appropriate skills to act as the school Technology Manager and that later she was able to use the enthusiasm of the two staff teams. Development would have moved much more slowly if it had all been top down or if the team had not been so willing to participate.

7 *Successful development needs adequate resourcing*

It is important for morale not to try to introduce major curriculum change on the cheap. This does not mean that you need to build the team a suite of rooms, but they do need to know that the essential resources are available and how they are going to be funded. Marion's brief to her two teams included working out their resource needs; it is sensible to get them to prioritise their requests into essential and desirable or at least an order of merit, and to discuss fully any problems. You can reasonably expect them to justify any requests for really expensive items, but in turn you need to be able to explain how you have prioritised the spending if you cannot provide all the items that they want.

8 *Try not to create an in-group as this builds up resentment*

Marion realised that the enthusiasm of the mini-enterprise team was setting it apart from the rest of the staff. While wishing to nurture their enthusiasm as it was critical to the success of the development, she did not want resentment to build up against the team. She also wanted to share some of the material benefits of TVEI more widely than with a small group. Buying some equipment that everyone would use, providing some Inset to raise awareness and setting up more than one team, opened up TVEI to the whole staff and at least went some way to dealing with what is always a difficult problem for any team manager.

9   *Always communicate the progress of an initiative*
In a busy school with a lot going on it is easy for people to lose track of things which do not immediately concern them. Putting out a progress report or taking a few minutes in a staff meeting as a briefing at least once in a half term will do a lot towards gaining and keeping goodwill. Marion was aware of this when she decided to use staff meeting time to remind staff of the financial benefits for them all of TVEI and this was also behind her decision to run an awareness raising session.

10   *You need to monitor and evaluate the development*
Marion organised Technology so that she and Kate King, the Technology manager, monitored progress, provided support for the task groups, organised Inset as needed and advised when problems emerged as they began to implement the course. The teams evaluated progress after each module and adapted the courses as they felt necessary. TVEI had a formal evaluation process written into its programme which made it easier to evaluate Technology than if they had had to devise their own scheme. Any curriculum development needs both monitoring and evaluation; arrangements for this should form part of the development plan right from its inception. (Advice about managing evaluation can be found in Chapter 9.)

Drafting a development plan

What is a development plan?

A development plan is your programme for carrying through an initiative. It is likely to cover a one, three or five year time span and will describe your philosophy and set out your programme of action for the period of the plan.

Why do you need a development plan?

1 It may be compulsory. Often you will have to produce a development plan because it is your method of accessing funds. You make a bid for funding in which you explain why you need the money and what you would do with it over a period of time. TVEI is an example of the kind of development for which you have to produce a development plan, otherwise your school will not get any money.

2 You need a development plan because it will help you structure an initiative. A development plan can be a useful management tool because it provides the framework for a change that you want to introduce.

How do you construct a development plan?

A development plan usually has the following sections:

1 *Where are we now?*
Start with an analysis of the present situation. Its purpose is to set the scene and to show your starting point. Although you may do a detailed analysis for yourself, what you include in the plan should be a brief statement of the most important points.

2 *Where do we want to go?*
This section of the plan sets out your aims and/or objectives. It describes what you want to do.
Your aim might be: To *introduce Technology into the school's curriculum.*
Your objectives could be: To *set up Technology courses in the Third and Fourth Years over a period of three years.*

3 *How are we going to get there?*
This section describes your strategy for carrying through the initiative. It gives your proposed timetable and the methods that you intend to use:

- *In Year One we shall set up a working party who will . . .*
- *In Year Two we shall run a pilot scheme . . .*
- *In Year Three we shall implement the initiative in all sections of the school . . .*

4   *What will it cost?*

Your plan has to consider all the resource implications of the initiative. Remember that resources are human, financial and locational. Can you staff the initiative? Will it need ancillary support? Does it have special reqirements in terms of rooms and facilities? What will it cost in terms of books, equipment, reprographics, time etc? These are just some of the items which will need to be costed out. You may find it difficult to give precise costs of all the items, but you must take into account that there will be a cost and whether it is likely to be substantial.

5   *What are our training needs?*

Curriculum development usually necessitates staff development. Your plan has to work out what the Inset requirements are likely to be for the whole period of its implementation. You need to take into account Inset for course development; relevant courses, visits, team building, skills training; possible retraining for individual staff etc. The costs of the Inset should be included with section 4 above.

6   *How shall we know when we have arrived?*

Your plan should include your arrangements for monitoring and evaluation. The monitoring is your short-term check or whether the targets that you have set are being met. The evaluation is your longer-term judgment as to how worthwhile the initiative has been for the school and for the pupils involved.

Case Study 8.2   *For reflection*
A DEVELOPMENT PLAN

TVEI TECHNOLOGY DEVELOPMENT PLAN   EASTMOUNT HIGH SCHOOL

1 THE CURRENT SITUATION
Eastmount High School is a girls' 11 - 18 comprehensive school of 769 pupils. Technology does not form part of its existing curriculum and the school lacks Technology facilities. At present no staff have specialist qualifications in Technology.

2 OVERALL AIM - what we hope to achieve by this initiative
Our aim is to develop Technology as part of the school's curriculum in accordance with TVEI and National Curriculum requirements.

OBJECTIVES
i)   To introduce Technological courses into the third and
fourth year by Year 2 of the development plan, using
existing expertise and facilities.
ii) To move towards the development and introduction of
courses more fully in accordance with the National
Curriculum etc as we build up expertise and equipment.

DEVELOPMENT STRATEGY
Overall management responsibility will be taken by the TVEI
Co-ordinator, Marion Parsons. The Technology Manager, Kate
King, will take responsibility for implementing the plan.

We envisage the introduction of Technology as a phased
development which will take us the whole five years of the
TVEI. It will need five years because the subject itself is
still developing and changing and because we lack facilities
and expertise. Thus full implementation of our programme is
dependent upon the county's equal opportunities building
programme, the purchase of necessary equipment and the
retraining of some staff.

In Year 1 we propose to send a Home Economics teacher on day
release to Eastmount College to learn to work in plastics,
so that we can expand the areas in which we can implement
Technology. We also hope to send a member of the Mathematics
Department to a twilight course on computer-aided design for
a term.
    In the first year of the plan, separate task groups of
staff will be set up to investigate ways in which we can
introduce courses of a technological nature. One task group
will be based on the Home Economics, Information Technology
and Art departments. These staff will plan the introduction
of a first form Technology course.
    A second task group, comprising teachers from a number of
subject disciplines, will consider how we can use the time
presently occupied by fourth form general courses so that
they can be developed into a modular Technology course.
    We hope that these courses will run at least as pilots by
Year 2 of the plan. We anticipate that these courses will be
reviewed and modified by the end of Year 3 to include work
in plastics and assignments more in line with the National
Curriculum requirements.

In Year 2 we hope to extend the first form course into the
second form and the fourth form course into the fifth form.
In Year 3 we hope to extend the junior course into the third
form. We also plan to set up a task group to investigate
possibilities within the sixth form curriculum for courses
which include some elements of Technology.
    Thus by Year 4 we hope that a progressive Technology
course will be in place covering years 1 - 5, and a pilot
scheme started for the sixth form. In Year 5 we shall review
and evaluate the initiatives in the light of current Key
Stage 4 and 16 - 19 requirements.

RESOURCE IMPLICATIONS
Staffing - This initiative will be sustained by .1 staff
release for the Technology manager to carry out the
development work. Cost = £1600 allocated from TVEI budget.

Technology teams of teachers for the new courses will have
to be staffed out of existing curriculum time - timetable
implications.
Ancillary staffing will be needed - TVEI budget £3000 pa.
Equipment - £2500 per year allocated out of TVEI equipment
budget (nb IT equipment will also be resourced separately
from TVEI and county IT programme). Some equipment should
also be funded from the county scheme when the building
programme is implemented.
Building - bid in to county building programme £500,000.
Reprographics - department allocation £400.
Consumables - department allocation £500.
Training costs - day release for 1 member of staff - county
pays from special fund. Twilight Computer Aided Design (CAD)
course funded from school GRIST external courses budget.
Inset for course teams - £700 pa from the Inset budget. This
will have to include attendance at courses.
Evaluation training and release time - £250.

TRAINING NEEDS
i) Skills training - day release for plastics training -
year 1; CAD twilight course - year 1. Possibility of further
skills training for other members of staff in subsequent
years as we become clearer what our needs will be.
ii) School based Inset for course development.
iii) Attendance by staff at consortium Technology Inset
sessions.
iv) Attendance at specific day courses within county or
external.
v) Management training for the Technology Manager.
vi) Training for the evaluator/s.
vii) Training for the ancillary staff. (This is likely to be
a problem as it does not come under school's Inset budget.)

MONITORING AND EVALUATION
i) Monitoring - targets will be agreed with the staff
involved and checked at six-monthly intervals by the
Technology Manager or the TVEI Co-ordinator as appropriate.
ii) The introduction of Technology is a TVEI initiative,
therefore it will contribute to the school's annual TVEI
evaluation following the procedure already established for
this.
iii) The school will evaluate its initiative at the end of
five years. A methodology will be established in
consultation with the County Adviser for Monitoring and
Evaluation.

Case Study 8.3   *For reflection*
SETTING TARGETS

Eastmount High School's TVEI support agreement illustrates the
way in which Marion Parsons, as the school's TVEI Co-ordinator,

set targets for her Technology manager. The support agreement also acts as a job description for Kate King.

SCHOOL EASTMOUNT HIGH SCHOOL

CURRICULUM AREA TECHNOLOGY

STAFF £1600 (·1 release)   ANCILLARY £3000   EQUIPMENT £2500

OBJECTIVES

To lead and support the development of Technology at Eastmount High School though:

1. Developing and delivering Technology courses for the First and Fourth Forms.

2. Organising and INSET programme for Technology.

3. Providing a training programme for the Technology Technician.

4. Liaising with the school's TVEI Co-ordinator and the Consortium Technology Curriculum Leader.

5. Attending meetings and conferences as required.

6. Contributing to TVEI evaluation.

Mrs K. King   Enhanced Teacher Mrs M. Parsons School Co-ordinator

Date 5.3.99   Miss M.B. Hardcastle Headteacher

Support agreements may be subject to changes due to unforseen circumstances such as change of personnel, or school objectives during the year. They will be used as a basis for evaluation and will be reviewed each half term with the TVEI Co-ordinator.

9 Managing evaluation

Managing monitoring and evaluation is a fairly new responsibility for a senior manager. This is because schools have not yet reached the stage where activities are evaluated as a matter of routine. For many of us evaluation is still a strange and rather threatening process, but really it is neither mysterious nor difficult, and within a short time it will have become an integral part of managing development. Evaluation will largely be school based. It will be your job as a senior manager to design an appropriate evaluation system. To help you deal with some of the problems that you may face, we have tried to provide answers to some of the key questions about monitoring and evaluation.

What is the purpose of monitoring and evaluation?

For many activities monitoring and evaluation is now a compulsory feature. If you are the school's TVEI Co-ordinator, evaluation will have been written into the LEA agreement with the Training Agency and will be a condition of funding. It will probably have involved you in writing a Co-ordinator's Overview of the previous year's work, and representatives from your local Consortium coming in to interview some of the staff involved in the TVEI initiatives, which received funding. They would be seeking information about whether targets had been met, and how the funding had been used. They may also have wanted information about the success of particular initiatives such as Technology, Balanced Science or Equal Opportunities. They were trying to build up a picture of how important a role TVEI had played in your school's development. The purpose of evaluation is therefore to find out about the progress of an initiative in order to inform future planning or decision making.

Defining the terms

Monitoring
A short-term immediate check on the delivery of development activities eg Are they meeting the planned targets? Monitoring is sometimes described as formative evaluation because, through its collection of data, it provides immediate feedback which can lead to alteration/improvement of the programme.

Evaluation
A longer-term judgment as to the worthwhileness of the development or activity. Is the programme meeting its general aims? What effect has the initiative had? What was the value of the development for the school or for its pupils?

When should monitoring and evaluation take place?

Monitoring should occur at regular intervals during the course of the development, because it provides information and opinions, which you will want to use in order to modify or improve a programme of activity. An end-of-term team meeting to review a new course will consider what has gone well and what the members found difficult to implement. You may want to sample pupil reactions to particular activities. This needs to be done while the activities are still fresh in the pupils' and the teachers' minds.

Formative evaluation is likely to be an annual event, with summative evaluation taking place in the last year of a long term initiative.

Who should carry out the evaluation?

The evaluator will usually be a teacher or group of teachers who are not themselves involved in the initiative being evaluated. The only time that it is likely to be impossible to find someone who is not a participant in the activity being evaluated is when the school has to evaluate its whole Inset programme. Then the evaluator/s should be selected from staff who are not on the Inset planning committee.

The aim of the person acting as the evaluator should be to hold back from making judgments, and collect the views of others in order to build up a picture that illuminates and informs. Once the information has been collected, the evaluator may choose whether or not to pass judgment on the evidence. Whoever you choose, however, the evaluator cannot escape some value judgments, whether his/her own or those of the people involved in the project. As long as the evaluator is aware of this it should not constitute a problem.

How should evaluation be carried out – what does it involve?

Evaluation is the collecting and analysis of relevant data about an activity such as curriculum development to discover whether it has met its objectives, what impact it has had and whether it has all been worthwhile. It is your task to design an evaluation system that suits both your school and the particular project or initiative which is to be evaluated. There is no master model to apply.

The evaluation needs to be carried out systematically and arrangements for it should be built into the development programme, so that it is known to all involved when and how the evaluation will operate. You will need to clarify what is to be evaluated and why; what information needs to be collected to serve the purpose, how it will be collected and over what period of time and how then it is to be analysed and by whom. There are a variety of possible approaches, all have their advantages and their drawbacks; your role as a manager is to make arrangements for deciding which are the most appropriate techniques to use.

Key techniques in carrying out evaluation

- Analysis of school documents – development plans, targets etc
- Written evaluation eg Co-ordinator's overview, evaluation questionnaire etc

- Group discussion – eg with the development team
- Interviews with some of the teachers involved – there are different ways you can organise these: formal, informal, structured, semi-structured
- Interviews with pupils
- Classroom observation of the initiative being implemented

What will the costs be?

Evaluation, like everything else, has inbuilt costs. It is important that you do not forget to budget for evaluation. Printing and paper costs, reprographics and ancillary support all contribute to the cost of evaluation. This is one of the reasons why it has to be included in the overall development plan. The largest single cost of evaluation will be the evaluator's time. You will need to arrange times when s/he can collect the information, analyse it and produce the report. This will involve buying supply cover, which is expensive. When you make your plans, think in terms of how much time it will need – hours, half days, days – and what it will add up to over the period of the project.

Our advice when planning the evaluation is to be realistic. Evaluation does not mean interviewing everyone who has participated in the activity. If you think it is important to get feedback from everyone, then use a questionnaire! What is actually important is to set up a system which produces the information needed but does not burden those involved too much.

How should the findings be disseminated?

The evaluator should produce a report summarising his/her findings. Its function is to disseminate and to feed back the findings to others. The report should be short, precise and easy to read. The evaluator needs to choose a format that has impact and to make the report interesting and relevant. Long, tedious documents simply gather dust on the staffroom table until someone throws them away in a tidying up session.

Issues and practices can be discussed in this kind of report, but individuals should not be identified. This is particularly important because you may wish to send a copy to governors or to the LEA.

Increasingly you will have to report to governors on the progress of an initiative and this is one way of avoiding having to write yet another report yourself! A copy to the LEA could help influence LEA policy making at the same time as demonstrating that you can cope with evaluation procedures.

Case Study 9.1   *For discussion*
**TWO APPROACHES TO EVALUATING
CURRICULUM DEVELOPMENT**

1   An evaluation questionnaire

Name of initiative:

Your role in the initiative:

What worked - why?

What did not work - why not?

What have you enjoyed about participating in this
development?

What have you found most difficult?

What do you think is needed to improve the design of this
course?

What do you think is needed to improve the delivery of
this course?

Do you think this development is achieving its purpose?

What do you think the value has been?

*Conditions to consider when completing this
questionnaire:*

*Resources - materials, time, staffing, space, expertise
available*

Conflicting/supporting initiatives

Support - LEA, TVEI, senior staff, colleagues

2 An evaluation planning proforma

INITIATIVE TITLE	EVALUATION STRATEGY	DATA TYPE	ANALYSIS METHOD
4th Form Mini Enterprise	Read school documents, target sheets, etc.	Written	Match targets to outcomes
	In depth interviews with 3 teachers	Interviews	Search for common themes / issues and for unexpected issues
	Sample reactions of pupils through a discussion session with one 'Company' in their lesson	Group discussion	Analyse reactions – Do the pupils understand the targets? Do they think that the targets have been achieved?

For discussion
1 How useful is each of these to the evaluator?
2 What else might you need?

Case Study 9.2   *For reflection*
SELF EVALUATION

TVEI evaluation – co-ordinator's overview

1 Our starting point

Eastmount High School is a girls' comprehensive school of 769 pupils. Before we entered TVEI, it would probably be fair to say that we had a fairly traditional approach to education. There were many areas of good practice, but few cross-curricular links and even fewer inter-institutional links. On the other hand, strong links with industry already existed, the majority of our Fifth Form took up the opportunity for work experience and several staff had enjoyed industrial placements. In terms of equal opportunities the majority of our pupils already studied at least one Science to 16, and 20% of our pupils studied three Sciences. There was no CDT, either wood or metal work in the curriculum nor the facilities to introduce them. Technological activities within the existing curriculum had not been defined, but Computer Awareness courses had been introduced into the Third and Fourth Form core. We had begun development work on our Fourth Form reports with a view to working towards a school record of achievement and were awaiting LEA guidance on how to proceed. PSE was being introduced into the school, working upwards from the First Form.

2   Curriculum development

There has been considerable curriculum development. We have introduced Balanced Science, Technology and PSE into the curriculum. Our curriculum decisions have been influenced by both the National Curriculum and TVEI and contrary to some earlier suggestions we have found no contradiction in terms in taking this approach. TVEI resourcing has made a considerable difference to curriculum development in the school, because it meant that we did not have to choose between the different developments, but were able to implement all of them in the first year of the initiative. TVEI thus served as a framework for a package of new courses. It also provided staff release to support both the Science and the Technology courses. This was important because these were major undertakings for us, which needed a lot of input from the departments concerned. Technology, for example, had to create its own syllabus. TVEI support enabled us to accept an invitation to participate in the local Balanced Science pilot scheme. TVEI has thus facilitated and supported curriculum development in the school.

3   Cross-curricular initiatives

TVEI has helped to provide an impetus for the development of cross-curricular links. There has been considerable activity, where in the past there was none. The two task groups who worked to develop Technology came from a number of different departments. Developing PSE brought together extra-departmental groups of staff, this time working as year teams. We were also pleased to see that developing Balanced Science increased the co-ordination between three separate Science subjects. A working party has also recently been established to look at Economic Awareness and it has decided to undertake a mapping exercise in the coming term. We regard this activity as a valuable and productive experience for the school.

4 Inset/staff training

TVEI has made a significant contribution to staff training at Eastmount High School, a variety of training opportunities has been provided.

1 All staff received at least one session of TVEI Inset through the consortium Inservice day last October. Difficulties in targeting so many staff at one time made this perhaps less effective than some of the other TVEI Inset sessions, but a real effort was made to provide an insight into TVEI and some training for all the teachers in the consortium's schools, and this was appreciated.
2 Training sessions were run by consortium or LEA Curriculum leaders. These were effective and well attended.
3 TVEI support enabled staff to attend external courses, eg the Head of Science attended six weekly sessions at Brunel University, and some members of the Mathematics department were able to attend the Logiston (spread sheet course) and helped to fund our own school-based Inset.

School Inset is planned as an integrated whole, not as LEATGS or TVEI which makes it difficult to disentange what is specifically TVEI, but it formed a significant part of the budget and allowed us to meet far more staff demands for training than otherwise would have been possible. We are concerned that a declining TVEI budget will limit future Inset activity in a period of continuing development.

5 Use of resources

The funding that we received from TVEI was used mainly to resource the new courses and to expand the use of IT in the school. This meant that we were able to introduce new courses which might not otherwise have been possible and yet not deprive other departments who could be resourced from capitation. TVEI funding also gave us some much-needed ancillary support. We consider ancillary support to be essential to the servicing of the new technological courses.

6   Inter-institutional links

1   The weekly Co-ordinators' meetings helped to create a viable consortium. We learnt to function as an effective planning group, and it was rare that one institution put its own interests before that of the consortium. In the current climate we consider this to have been an important achievement.

2   The subject co-ordinators have also benefited from the twice-termly meetings, which have facilitated the exchange of ideas and discussion and lead to visits between individual schools.

3   We have benefited from participating in the LEA pilot scheme for Balanced Science. The staff involved in the project have now developed good links with two other schools in the pilot scheme. There has been some joint Inset for curriculum development and regular visits between the three schools.

7   Industry links

We have tried to change the emphasis of our industry links by trying to involve two or three firms in supporting our mini-enterprising, including joining our curriculum development team. This is evolving slowly and we are not displeased with progress so far. Hopefully next year when a member of staff receives timetable release to co-ordinate industry links, this initiative will gain momentum.

8   Overview

For Eastmount High School TVEI has been a very important facilitator. Project funding has made possible a much higher level of development than would otherwise have been the case. It has also demonstrated the importance of staff release to curriculum development, because where development was supported by staff release, much more was achieved than where it was not. It also provided challenging management experience for the subject co-ordinators, who had to set and meet targets, plan, implement, monitor and evaluate development and give leadership to their subject team. Even more important, the TVEI development plan provided a coherent framework through which to co-ordinate activities which otherwise would have been piecemeal.

Marion Parsons TVEI Co-ordinator

The case study above is a TVEI Co-ordinator's Self Evaluation. It is a part of the school's annual formative evaluation process for the TVEI initiative and is the result of the Co-ordinator's discussions with the staff involved and her own assessment of the progress being made.

Ways in which self-evaluation can be useful to a school

A self-evaluation paper about an initiative can be a very useful tool for the curriculum manager. It is part of the monitoring process for the development – contributing to formative evaluation. While not pretending to be objective, it is an opportunity for the manager to stand back and assess an initiative. It helps him/her analyse:

- what is going well;
- whether all parts of the initiative are equally successful;
- how far targets are being met;
- what adjustments to the programme would be beneficial.

It also provides a useful basis for external evaluation of a project as it gives them the school's perception of how the initiative is proceeding.

Case Study 9.3   *For reflection*
MONITORING INSET AT BESTWICK PARK

This is how the Senior Management Team at Bestwick Park went
about collecting data about Inset in order to evaluate Inset activity
over the previous year and help the school plan how to organise its
Inset for the following year.

1   Setting up the inset data base

<u>BESTWICK PARK HIGH SCHOOL</u>

INSET Record

MONTH May

STAFF Mrs Michael, Mr Blake, Mrs Croft

AREA		
	PSE	Appraisal
	LMS	National Curriculum
	IT	Evaluation
	GCSE	Team Teaching
	A level	Research
	Profiling	Course development ✓ Humanities
	Specific	Careers
	....	....

TITLE OF INSET Humanities Development

LENGTH ½ Day

PLACE		
	External	Consortium
	County	Class
	School ✓	....

FUNDING		
	GRIST ✓	ESG Diversification
	JSA	TVEI
	County	Staff cover
	None	....

TYPE		
	Twilight	Baker Day
	Residential	School based & focused

LEADER		
	Adviser	HOD
	Self	Advisory teacher visiting
	Home ✓	....

SUPPLY NEEDED (days) . 4 periods ......

2   Analysing the data

Where did our Inset take place?

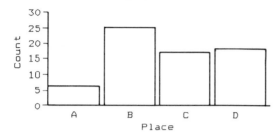

KEY:

A : Consortium
B : County
C : External
D : School

What were the main areas of activity?

KEY:

A : Appraisal
B : Assessment
C : Curriculum
D : Curriculum 16–19
E : Equal Opportunities
F : Equal Opps
G : Industry Links
H : IT
I : LMS
J : Management
K : PSE
L : Specific (subjects)
M : Specific, PSE
N : Technology
O : Work Experience

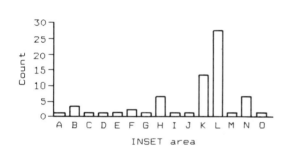

How was the school's Inset funded?

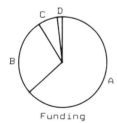

A : GRIST/LEATGS   62%
B : TVEI   28%
C : County   8%
D : Others   2%

10 Managing staff development (1) Inset

Managing staff development and Inset has become an important senior management task. The onset of GRIST brought more money into schools, along with a bidding system which needed careful management. Since this time, the number of initiatives for which staff need further training and development has increased markedly. As the amount of Inset expanded, the nature of provision changed. While attendance at external courses did not cease, it began to be supplemented by school-based and school-focused training, and by visits from advisory teachers or area curriculum leaders. Appraisal, too, began to feature on the staff development programme.

Organisation of school-based inservice ('Baker' days) and co-ordination of the wide range of Inset activity emerged as a senior management function in many schools. If you have the role of Inset co-ordinator, you could have one of several possible titles: Inset Co-ordinator, Deputy Head (Staff Development), School Development Officer, or Professional Tutor. Whatever your title, the job of managing the Inset cycle carries a heavy and challenging workload and demands a high level of management skill (Figure 8).

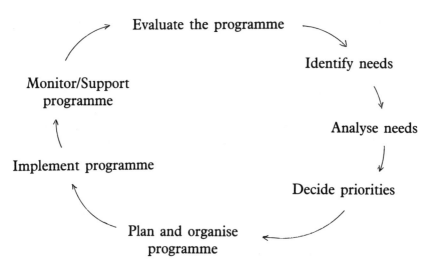

Evaluate the programme

Identify needs

Monitor/Support
programme

Analyse needs

Implement programme

Decide priorities

Plan and organise
programme

Based on O'Sullivan, Jones and Reid *Staff Development in Secondary Schools*

Figure 8 *The Inset Cycle*

Case Study 10.1   *For reflection*
WHAT AN INSET CO-ORDINATOR NEEDS

This list was produced by a working party at Bestwick Park High School. It gives the skills and personal qualities required by an Inset Co-ordinator.

Skills
Listening
Negotiating
Chairmanship
Organisational/administrative
Ability to enthuse
Ability to facilitiate
Communication
Creativity
Flair

Personal qualities
Tact/sensitivity
Motivation and willingness to
  work hard
Sense of humour
Versatility
Enthusiasm
Organisational tenacity
Stamina/resilience/drive
Optimism
Flexibility

The following quotation from the TRIST Handbook *Managing Professional Development and Inset* may help you appreciate why these skills and qualities are needed:

> *From the early days it has become more than obvious that the Inset Co-ordinator is more than just an administrator and facilitator for staff. Although we may all have a different understanding of the terms, we have identified the following different roles for the Inset Co-ordinator.*
>
> **Counsellor**   *The Inset Co-ordinator will be seen to have power and to some extent will be seen to appraise teachers individually as well as assessing their needs. This hierarchical role will have to be handled very carefully if the inevitable tensions are to be minimised. For many Co-ordinators this will be a new and difficult role to play.*
>
> **Motivator**   *It will often be the responsibility of the Co-ordinator to motivate staff towards realistic self-assessment of their own developmental needs. On occasion the Co-ordinator will have to raise the confidence of staff who are experiencing difficulties.*
>
> **Innovator**   *The Co-ordinator will have a responsibility to encourage staff to become involved in new educational initiatives, similarly s/he may need to encourage the school's senior management team to move the school in certain, sometimes threatening, directions.*
>
> **Mentor**   *The complexity of the role of Co-ordinator arises here where the Inset Co-ordinator, often in a hierarchical position, must also be seen to be a successful practitioner, able to share the experiences of classroom interaction. The credibility of the Co-ordinator will be in most danger in this aspect of his/her role.*
>
> **Monitor**   *The Co-ordinator will need to monitor the progress of teachers in a non-threatening way and will need to monitor the overall programme of Inset undertaken by the school.*
>
> **Evaluator**   *The Co-ordinator will have to evaluate not only the progress of staff development in the school, but also the value of the Inset undertaken by staff.*
>
> **Administrator**   *The more obvious role of the Co-ordinator is to liaise with the district co-ordinators etc and to administer the Inset programme.*

Facilitator As part of the administrative role the Co-ordinator will need to help teachers to discover the appropriate Inset to be undertaken and to arrange for suitable supply cover. The Co-ordinator has a major facilitating role when arranging in-house Inset.

How to get started – a checklist for an Inset Co-ordinator

If you are given responsibility for the school's Inset programme, the following checklist could provide a useful starting point. The answers to these questions could help you identify the areas where you should concentrate your attention.

1 Did you receive any training to do this work, or any guidance?
2 How is the needs appraisal perceived – as developmental, as assessment of deficiencies or simply as something required by the LEA before it will grant your school any money?
3 Who is responsible for carrying it out – you, a staff development committee or what?
4 How were the staff prepared? Was there any form of awareness raising or did you just give them all a questionnaire at the end of a staff meeting?
5 Do you use a range of methods of needs identification or only one?
6 Does your chosen method provide sufficient information ie tell you about institutional, group and individual needs?
7 What use is made of past information or do you start from scratch again every year?
8 Is there a staff development profile for each member of staff? If there is, how easy is it to use? Do you have computerised staff records?
9 What do you do with the information after you have collected it? How do you go about analysing it?
10 How do you determine priorities?
11 Who makes the decisions – you, a committee, the senior management team, or the Head?
12 Is your programme on-going? How does one year's Inset link to the following year?

13   How are your Inset decisions communicated to the staff?
14   What forms of Inset are mainly used in the school – external courses, school based activities, use of advisory teachers or curriculum leaders, team teaching, a mixture? Has there been any change in the main forms of Inset used in the last couple of years?
15   How do you evaluate the programme – questionnaire, personal interviews, outside evaluators or what?

Managing the Inset cycle

Carrying out a needs appraisal

The Inset funding arrangements require schools 'to ensure that appropriate account is taken of the expressed needs and views of teachers, schools and colleges'. DES Circular 6/86. This means that schools have to carry out some form of needs appraisal in order to make their annual Inset bid. As the Inset Co-ordinator you will have to gather and interpret the required data. This is a complex task because there will be more than one level in the school at which development can be desirable.

1   *Find out what information your school already has and what has been done about it*
Your predecessor should already have a lot of information on file. Most schools have now operated GRIST/LEATGS for some years and will have gathered a lot of information, particularly if staff questionnaires have been used; you should be able to build on that information. If you want to make yourself really unpopular, all you have to do is to keep battering hard-worked staff with yet another questionnaire when the school has not done anything about the one that they filled in last time!

It is counterproductive to spend too much time identifying needs if that causes delay in meeting them. If it is well done, however, the exercise of identifying needs is itself a form of Inset which raises staff awareness.

2   *Establish who the target audience is*
It will be necessary to identify needs for three different groups:

- *The school as a whole* Whole school review could indicate a need for training for the whole staff in such things as profiling skills or management training or indicate a need to raise awareness in a sensitive area such as multicultural education.
- *Sections of the school* Each section of the school will have its own particular needs, eg a department might need to prepare for the introduction of a new syllabus or do some curriculum development.
- *Individual needs either for professional training or for career development* Individual members of staff will want to build upon strengths and look for ways to improve their performance in the classroom or develop new skills such as expertise in computing. Some staff will be looking for Inset which will help them to further their own career, eg management training.

3 *Decide the methods that you are going to use*

The list below – which is not intended to be comprehensive – gives some possible approaches:

- Use a professionally developed model, eg GRIDS or DION for whole school or departmental review.
- Design your own questionnaire/s. Questionnaires gather a lot of information quickly. They are useful if you want departments to bid for part of the Inset budget or if you are looking for ways of getting information about individual needs.
- Personal interviews. A personal interview is a good way of discovering individual professional and career needs. This takes a lot of time so it works best if it is built into your school appraisal system or if the interviews are carried out by the staff development team rather than by one person.

Analysing needs

Whatever methods you have used to acquire data, it will now need to be analysed. One way of grouping needs could be by the three categories of development – whole school needs, group needs and individual needs. But it is more likely that you will want to start by making some sort of list of the requests that indicate the number of individual teachers or groups who have asked for a particular form of training. This will give an indication of whether there are some areas where a lot of staff feel that they need training. It will also show you where there are gaps in awareness; a lack of requests for development in an area where you know the school is not strong could indicate a need for consciousness raising.

You will have to cost the requests. Here you will be looking at the overall cost of meeting all the demands, but you will also need to assess just how greedy each department has been and to check how much Inset a particular person or department had last year.

It is very likely that you will find that the list of requests is much greater than your Inset budget will allow. You will then have to decide what your priorities are. Once you have completed the analysis you should have established a pattern of demand.

Setting up an Inset committee

Participating in Inset planning by serving on a Staff Development or Inset Committee is useful for staff who want to extend their experience of cross-curricular or whole school activities. The programme is generally more valued by staff if they are involved in its construction and they are also more likely to understand how their personal needs fit into the overall pattern of Inset provision and development within the school.

Deciding who should serve on the Inset Committee may cause you some headaches. Should it be nominated, self-selecting or democratically elected? The method of selection that seems to produce the most effective working party is to use a mixed system. Start by asking for volunteers. This will indicate who are the enthusiasts (or the ambitious). After a few days, analyse the kind of team that would then be created. How representative is it of different levels of experience and subjects? You do not want to reject a person who has volunteered to give up time to help staff development, but if the committee consists mainly of members of one Faculty, you may need to suggest that it sends only one or two representatives. It is difficult for people to give of their best if they are involved in too many activities, so discourage the committee 'groupies'. Deflecting people that you do not want takes tact, but it is part of the job. You are likely to have some spaces left so if people you think would be valuable workers for this committee have not yet come forward, it is now time to have a word with them. This also gives you the opportunity to balance the team, eg senior to junior staff, a mix of departments, some pastoral representatives etc. It is a good idea to look at your staff development records to see who is not serving on any other working party and if possible to include someone for whom membership of this group would be good development experience. Remember not to make the team too big or, as with any team or working party with too many members, it will have difficulty in doing its job.

The powers of the Inset committee will vary from school to school, but what you want is to provide a mechanism that enables the group to meet regularly to work with you to plan, organise and monitor the Inset programme. The draft proposals of an Inset Committee are usually submitted to the senior management group for approval.

Although leading the supporting a Staff Development Committee is a major task in itself, it can be very rewarding and has two distinct advantages for you:

1 It gives you a team that works directly to you. This is rare at senior management level.
2 It can actually do a lot of the work involved in running Inset which you would otherwise be doing yourself.

Deciding your priorities

When you decide your priorities you will need to ask yourself a number of questions:

- What activities from the previous programme should you retain?
- What are the major gaps thrown up by your analysis of needs and demands?
- What does the school see as its immediate priorities?
- How do the school's priorities relate to LEA priorities?
- Where do national priorities fit into your scheme?

It is no longer the case that an institution can simply decide what its priorities are and then write itself a development programme. Increasingly, a lot of Inset is becoming externally determined – either by the DES or by the LEA. These externally imposed priorities may coincide with the school's own priorities, but it is likely that they will need to take precedence over any previous development programme you may have and almost certainly speed it up. Preparation for the GCSE or National Curriculum had to take priority in the years they were first being introduced. Thus a major task will be to marry up not only individual and group and whole school priorities but the school's priorities with national and LEA priorities.

Budgeting for Inset

Organising the school's Inset programme means that you have to work within a budget. The size of this budget varies enormously from one LEA to another, but the most usual figure is about one supply day per member of staff. This means that you will need to cost each item on the programme. Costs could include: fees to speakers or providing agencies; expenses such as travel; resource needs; hire of premises if you want to go off site; cost of lunch, coffee etc. The largest single expense is usually the cost of supply cover to release staff from teaching their classes. The most costly forms of Inset are to take a group of staff off site to a residential session or to buy in external agencies to run a course or Baker day for your school. But this does not mean you should not use them. Do not simply go for the cheapest form of provision each time as it may not achieve your aims. Rather, you will have to set the cost of these activities against what you expect to gain or achieve. You will have to assess whether you have enough in-house talent to run the event or course without having to buy in and, if you do so, whether your staff will respond better to someone they know because that person would carry more conviction that an outside 'expert', who may not have been in a classroom for many years. If the issue is sensitive – either because it is unpopular with some staff or seen as a threat – it may well be wiser to use an outside agency in the first instance. You also need to look at how one expensive item will affect the rest of the programme. If you do decide to plan an expensive activity eg arranging for the senior management team to have a weekend at a hotel to plan a major initiative, how do you justify this to the rest of the staff, if it means that you are having to reject most of their bids? Your programme will need to be cost effective within your overall budget.

Planning your programme

You have created a list of priorities; now you need to decide for each priority area how much provision should be made, when the Inset should occur and what form it should take. Your aim should be to produce a year's programme which can be published for the staff so that everyone can see not only what they get but also the overall pattern of provision.

Drawing up the school's Inset bid

To get the money that the LEA will allocate to your school under the LEATGS system, the school will probably have to submit an Inset Proposal. This means listing, explaining and costing each individual item in your programme. As Inset Co-ordinator you will probably be given the task of drafting the bid. You will have been sent the list of national and LEA priorities with the bid documents. If your plans reflect these priorities, the money you want will be granted much more easily than if they do not. Do read the accompanying notes carefully as they sent out the ground rules for drafting the bid. If you ignore them you could cost your school money and time and probably lose yourself a lot of goodwill as well. Notice particularly when the deadline is, because you will need time to discuss the draft document with the Head/senior management team and maybe amend it before it is sent off to the LEA. If the document is to be typed by the school office you should allow about a week for this.

Implementing and supporting the programme

It is your task as Inset Co-ordinator to ensure that the Inset programme works. Your role is that of a facilitator and counsellor. You have to see that any group or individual allocated time or money have sorted out what they want to do, otherwise you may find that an Inset activity has not happened because nobody has done anything about organising it. A group may need support or guidance in how it structures the session or need you to liaise with the Deputy in charge of administration to provide facilities or the supply cover that they need. You may also need to attend some sessions or parts of sessions, especially of cross-curricular Inset, not just to check how they are going, but to provide practical advice about possibilities.

Individuals may also come to you for advice. They may want to know what training is available in order to improve a particular skill or be seeking counselling about career development. They may have found a course that interests them and want to know how they should go about applying for it, or how the fees and expenses should be met.

Evaluating Inset

You will have to decide the most appropriate method of evaluation for your school's Inset programme. It will be used internally to assess the success of the programme for the school so that you can see what elements need change or modification, and it will be used externally as most LEAs now expect you to submit some form of evaluation report. When GRIST first started schools tended to carry out evaluation through questionnaires, but this is no longer regarded as sufficient, so what should you do? Chapter 9 on *Managing Evaluation* aims to help you clarify what evaluation entails and should give you some ideas about possible approaches. What is important is that the system that you set up does not become yet another paper-heavy burden for staff. Remember, you do not have to evaluate all aspects of Inset each year – be selective. This kind of issues which would need to be addressed would include:

- Analysis of the effectiveness of individual events and of the overall programme;
- Did the activities meet the needs that were perceived?
- Were the activities successful in themselves?
- How many of the staff were involved in the programme?
- How much of the programme was school-based activity and how much was through attendance at external courses?
- What were the outcomes of the activities?

Reporting back

The evaluation report is likely to be seen in full only by two small groups of staff – the Staff Development Committee and the Senior Management Team. Both will use it as the basis of next session's planning. It is also the source of information for whatever form of report has to be submitted to the LEA though material may have to be extracted and a specific form filled in. It is unlikely, because it is a technical and possibly lengthy document, to be presented in full to the whole staff, yet they need to be kept in the picture about progress and consulted regularly.

Reporting to staff is important if the Inset programme is to be owned by them rather than imposed upon them. A regular slot in any staff information bulletin could serve this purpose. If this does not exist, you may need to produce a short Inset News, eg with the main points of the evaluation or short reports of activities and updates on the current programme. As with any written information, if you want it to be read – keep it short, never longer than one side of paper.

An occasional input into a staff meeting can be an effective way of giving information or consulting colleagues, eg should we provide a staff lunch on the Inservice day?

Case Study 10.2   *Exemplar*
BESTWICK PARK DRAFT INSET
PROGRAMME

This is the programme for the Autumn Term drawn up by Inset Co-ordinator, Michael Wade, and the Staff Development Committee.

AUTUMN TERM DRAFT INSET PROGRAMME

Inservice (Baker) days
1 Wed Sept 3rd. Awareness raising day on a whole school issue –
Profiling. Outside speakers (County Profiling Team) Staff lunch
provided.
2 Mon Nov 4th. Departmental Curriculum Development Day – school
based in-house curriculum development. Staff to decide whether
lunch should be provided.

Departmental Inset
1 Mathematics Dept. Coursework in the National Curriculum. 3
supply days to be used in Oct to provide 2 mornings Inset for the
whole dept. Consecutive mornings if possible.
2 Science Dept. Developing balanced Science. 3 supply days to be
used for 2 sessions in Nov.
3 German Dept. Preparation of new AL syllabus. 1 supply day in
Sept.
4 Economics Dept. Increasing Economic Awareness. 1 supply day
in Nov.

Cross curricular Inset
1 Technology Development Team. 2½ supply days to be used in Oct
for curriculum development. (long afternoon 1 - 5pm, tea provided).
2 Integrated Humanities. 1½ supply days for 2 - 3 staff to have
2 half days, 1 day in Sept. 1 day in Dec.
3 Profiling Working Party. 2 supply days afternoons, Oct and Nov.

Approved courses
1.1 member of the numanities Dept. to attend the county support
day for the pilot project (Oct).
2 Head of Music: Day course - Music in TVEI (Nov.)
3 Head of RE: Day course - Comparative Religion (Dec.)
4.1 member of the Modern Languages Dept. Day course: The use of
the media in language teaching.
nb six supply days are to be allocated this term for courses.
Courses not yet known about are to be considered on merit.

Twilight courses offered in school:
1 Middle Management: 6 sessions, weekly Weds Sept 20th onwards.
4.00 - 6.00 pm. Led by Inset Co-ordinator. Some outside speakers.
Tea provided.
2 Improving PSE Skills - 6 sessions. Tues from Spet 11th, led by
Pastoral Deputy Head. Some outside speakers. Tea provided (max 25).

Evaluation
½ day supply for evaluator.

SOME POINTS TO CONSIDER ABOUT THIS PROGRAMME

The team have had to balance whole school priorities against
departmental requests. They have addressed this partly through their
use of the school's two Inservice days for the Autumn Term, using
one for a whole school issue, bringing in the county profiling
team to provide information and some practical training in
constructing profiles and arranging that follow up work can be
done by a working party, to which they have allocated supply
time. They have used the second Inservice day to meet the majority
of departmental requests for time for curriculum development. The
curriculum development work is very important for the school, but
so many requests can be very expensive in supply time and extremely
disruptive to lesson continuity, so it made sense to meet a lot of
the requests through an Inservice day when there are no lessons.

They have decided to provide lunch for the Profiling session as it
provides an opportunity to continue discussion and to talk to
speakers and they perceive it as an integral part of that day.
They would prefer not to spend money on lunch for the second
Inservice day as it was not essential and the money could pay
for 3 or 4 more supply days cover for other Inset activities
which have not found a place on the programme. As the issue was
sensitive they have sensibly decided that it should be decided
by the staff at the next staff meeting.

They have grouped the Inset into categories rather than simply
providing a calendar of events, because this way it is easier for
staff to understand the thinking behind the programme. They have
however allocated a rough time for the Inset so that it does not
all bunch together, but left to the Deputy in charge of daily
administration the task of deciding the precise day.

Department Inset has been allocated for major new curriculum
initiatives, which needed time over and above the Inservice day
or for sub-departments who did not receive an individual allocation
of time on the Inservice day. German, for example, participated in
the Modern Languages Inset on Nov 4th, but also needed some time to
prepare a new syllabus. Similarly time has been allocated for
specific cross-curricular initiatives.

Six supply days have been allocated for attendance at external
courses. This will clearly not cover every request. Indeed not all

the courses approved by the committee will receive supply. What has been agreed is that staff will cover some courses and the Deputy Head will use the six days flexibly to relieve the burden of cover so that it could be possible either for two members of staff to attend an important course or for more than one member of staff to go on a course on the same day. Notice that the committee has approved day courses for the heads of very small departments who have difficulty doing school-based Inset.

The programme for the Autumn will use nearly half the annual Inset budget. This is because the school has learnt that it is much less expensive to support Inset in the Summer Term as 5th and U6th forms are on public examination leave for much of the term. So the budget is not divided equally into thirds, rather the largest share of the budget is allocated to the longest term.

Some twilight courses have been arranged for groups of staff who want to improve personal skills. This is a new venture for the school. The needs analysis showed up a lot of demand for these courses.. External courses in school time would have meant that only one or two people could have been granted funding or release so the committee decided to offer some twilight school-based training, monitor what the take-up and reaction were and review the position when they planned the next inset programme.

The committee is conscious of the need to evaluate the Inset programme and has allowed half a day supply time per term, which the evaluator can either use for sampling or for working on the evaluation report.

Case Study 10.3   *For reflection*
PLANNING AN INSERVICE DAY

Working paper from Michael Wade, Inset Co-ordinator at Bestwick Park High School for discussion at senior management meeting.

INTRODUCING APPRAISAL

1 OBJECTIVES
We need to approach this issue with care. Appraisal is an extremely sensitive area. Most staff are not well informed about it and may feel threatened by the whole idea. Our objectives should be:
a) To raise awareness by providing information.
b) To provide an opportunity for full discussion so that staff can air their fears and concerns.

2 METHODS
There are various possibilities, eg
a) 'In-house'. It would be quite possible to set up a day centred round our own staff. Mrs Gatlin had experience of introducing appraisal in her previous post and could deal with the theory and general mangement issues. Then we could centre on the Humanities Faculty, who have over the last

year or so introduced their own scheme. We could link into this some of the video material now available as we could borrow it from the LEA.
Advantages It would have credibility with the staff as the people involved are known and are classroom practitioners. It would be inexpensive and easy to organise.
Disadvantages It could create problems for us. It could become personal as we should have to deal personally with the feelings aroused and hostility to a scheme could turn into hostility to individuals. On the other hand, people may not feel free to voice their criticisms where the Headteacher is seen to be supporting it by leading the training day, or it could be seen as imposing one faculty's scheme on the whole school.
b) Buy in an outside agency to run the day for us. There are now a number of agencies whom we could book, who would do the whole thing for us.
Advantages It is much less personal so it might be easier for staff to talk freely. It is also easy to manage as once we have made the booking we can leave the content of the day to the agency.
Disadvantages Will it carry conviction? The course tutors are often people who have escaped from the classroom or have not taught for a very long time. It is quite expensive and we cannot be certain how much control we would have over the content and philosophy. We should certainly check that the programme of any agency we use is in line with LEA current thinking on appraisal.
c) A mixed system - integrate some outsiders into a school-focused programme. We could invite a head from the neighbouring LEA, where appraisal already operates, to talk about how it has worked in her/his school. If we did this I would also want to invite one or two teachers from the school so that staff could get grassroots opinion as well as management view. We might prefer to bring in our own Link Adviser to talk about how the LEA sees appraisal working here. This could help allay fears about it being judgmental. We could bring in representatives from industry to tell us what they do and we could explore similarities and differences between schools and industry. I have enough contacts to arrange this quite easily. We could use all or any of this, dependent on how much you feel staff can absorb in one session.
Advantages We could control the programme more easily than if we use an agency and could provoke a positive response.
Disadvantages It would take the most organisation. We could not be sure about how the information would be delivered as we would be including some people who are not experienced speakers.

3 FOLLOW UP
Whatever approach to the actual day we choose, we also need to clarify how we intend to follow up the training day. I think it is important to set up a working party who will design an appraisal scheme for us and we need to start thinking about how we shall provide the necessary training so that we can operate appraisal. It would therefore seem sensible to take some time in the final session of the day to set up the mechanisms for a working party and to explain how we intend to move forward.

After discussion at a senior management meeting, it was decided that a mixed system should be used. This is the draft programme that Mike Wade then produced:

BESTWICK PARK HIGH SCHOOL

INSERVICE DAY PROGRAMME June 16th

Subject: Appraisal   Location: Staff Common Room

Coffee will be served at 8.45 a.m. The first session will begin at 9.00 a.m.

Introduction: Mrs Gatlin 9.00 - 9.15
Session 1 9.15-10.45 How appraisal works in Middlehampton. The experience of a high school in the neighbouring LEA. Andrew Lively, Head of Middlehampton High School, will lead this session, together with Barbara Baker, who is head of mathematics at the school. This session will include the opportunity to ask questions.
Coffee 10.45 - 11.00
Session 2 11.00 - 12.00 Activity based on the first session.
Lunch 12.00 - 1.00 Outside if the weather remains good, otherwise in the dining room.
Session 3 1.00 - 2.00 Video of how appraisal operates, followed by questions.
Session 4 2.00 - 3.15 Simulation led by members of the Humanities Dept. followed by discussion groups.
Plenary 3.15 - 3.30
(NB Mr Lively and Mrs Baker will be with us for the whole day's programme.)

Case Study 10.4   *For reflection*
MICHAEL WADE'S CHECKLIST FOR AN INSERVICE DAY

1 Book speakers and confirm this in writing. Include a map showing where the school is located.
2 Write to or preferably phone speakers to brief them about our requirements for the day. Firm up programme at this stage.
3 Make sure that any outside speakers understand the LEA's system of claiming their fees and expenses. This prevents trouble later.
4 Check room requirements for the day. Will small rooms for group activities be needed as well as the main conference hall?
5 Check what equipment will be needed - flip chart, video, OHP etc.

6   Check the catering arrangements. It is important that
coffee and lunch slot neatly into the day's programme.
Giving the caterer a copy of the timetable of events could
prevent arguments later.
7   Publish the programme well in advance - on the staff
noticeboard or in the staff news bulletin, so that people
have plenty of time to absorb the information and are clear
what is happening.
8   Give a personal copy of the programme to Hd and check
what role s/he wants in the proceedings.
9   Check that the caretaker has a copy of the programme so
that there is no problem about access to rooms or equipment.
10 Remember to check the day before that all the equipment
etc actually works!

11 Managing staff development (2)

What is staff development?

If you are given responsibility for managing staff development, it will involve you in much more than simply co-ordinating the school's Inset programme. A definition of staff development is provided in the Case Study 11.1 below, which describes the policy adopted by Bestwick Park High School.

Case Study 11.1   *For discussion*
BESTWICK PARK HIGH SCHOOL STAFF
DEVELOPMENT POLICY

Definition
Staff development is a deliberate and continuing process which supports the growth both of individuals and the institution in which they work.

Staff Development ⟨ Developing the Curriculum ⟩ Enhancing the
                    Developing the Individual → quality of teaching
                    Developing the Institution and learning.

It results from a planned programme of learning opportunities determined by the identification of present and anticipated needs for enhancing job satisfaction through greater effectiveness.

Aims
To foster continuing professional development.
To support curriculum development.
To enable forward planning and policy development.
To support management of change.
To support teachers in developing strategies to respond to rapid change.
To establish a process of review and evaluation.
To facilitate career development.

Objectives
The objectives of our staff development programme will be to set up the processes which are concerned with achieving our aims. These should take place within the context of open and continuous dialogue and shared involvement.

Organisation
Staff development will be managed by the Deputy Head responsible for staff development, who will work in close association with the Inset Co-ordinator and a Staff Development Committee.

Delivery
Staff development will be delivered through Inset activities such as courses, conferences, seminars, workshops, job rotation or secondments.

Our programme for staff development should also include other kinds of learning opportunities such as appraisal, collaborative working, shadowing, team group meetings, joint planning etc.

Evaluation
Staff development at Bestwick Park is evaluated in a number of ways:
The level and areas of activity are monitored by the recording and evaluating of Inset data.
The Inset programme is a part of the school management plan which is reviewed annually by the senior management team.
Staff questionnaires and individual interviews.
Review by the staff development committee.

For discussion

1 How do the activities and learning opportunities mentioned in the Bestwick Park policy statement relate to the staff development activities undertaken in your own school?

2 Does your school have a staff development policy? Who would need to be involved in drafting and approving it?

Two key areas of managing staff development are *Introducing appraisal* and the role of *Counsellor*. These aspects are examined in detail below.

A definition of teacher appraisal

Teacher appraisal is a structured, agreed and confidential procedure within a school and a Local Education Authority, which assists the two way collection, sharing, evaluation and application of information about a teacher at work. The purpose of this is to assist that teacher in improving his or her performance as a teacher.

(William J Haykin and Anthony Pierce
CCDU *Teacher Appraisal Project*)

If you are the school's Inset Co-ordinator or the Deputy Head in charge of Staff Development, the likelihood is that introducing appraisal will fall to your lot. As a senior manager you are probably already an experienced change agent. The issue here is whether – and to what degree – introducing appraisal differs from planning and implementing any other whole school development. In fact introducing appraisal is a management of change situation and you could apply the Rank Xerox Management of Change Model to working out how to approach this issue.

Where appraisal differs from other management of change situations is in its extreme sensitivity. It is a particularly difficult change to manage – a real challenge for any manager. This is because of the hostility to appraisal that has existed for many years among teachers who have not experienced it. Surveys have found that people who have been involved in appraisal are positive about its benefits, but that it is the change most feared and opposed by staff who have had little contact with it. Thus, not only will you have to work out an appropriate structure for the change, you will also face a more than usually difficult task when you try to convince staff that they want to participate in the process.

To convince staff you will have to demonstrate the benefits of appraisal, so you will need to be clear what these are for both the school and for the individual teachers.

Some benefits of appraisal for the school
- It provides more accurate information for reference purposes.
- It informs Inset policy-making decisions.
- It helps the school to see where a new or changed role or assignment would help the professional development of the teacher concerned.
- Developing and motivating teachers through appraisal helps improve the delivery of the curriculum.
- It helps to identify potential.

Some benefits of appraisal for teachers
- It provides greater confidence and improved morale for individual teachers, thus enhancing job satisfaction.
- It provides an opportunity to discuss training needs and how they can best be met.
- It provides an opportunity for individuals to discuss career development.
- It helps in identifying areas of strength and successful practice.
- It helps identify areas of weakness and provides practical help in overcoming them.

Remember, if appraisal is to fulfil its purpose, it should always be *developmental* not *judgmental*.

Case Study 11.2 describes how one senior manager approached the task of introducing appraisal.

Case Study 11.2   *For reflection*
PLANNING APPRAISAL

Bestwick Park High School has decided to introduce appraisal.

1 The decision is taken

Some of the management team, particularly Mike Wade, the Staff Development Officer, are very positive about appraisal. Others are much more apprehensive, concerned about staff reaction and unconvinced of any benefits. Mr Brown, the Pastoral Deputy, is particularly hostile. He is overwhelmed with his present workload and cannot see why they should take on yet another new initiative. The Headteacher, Brenda Gatlin, has decided to go ahead on the grounds that she herself strongly supports appraisal. She believes that once it is in place a lot of the opposition will melt away. There have now been sufficient pilot schemes to provide models from which to work. The school would have to introduce appraisal within a year or so anyway, because it is already in government legislation and has begun to appear in LEA priorities. Mrs Gatlin feels that she would prefer to develop a scheme that suits her school's needs and that might influence LEA planning, rather than drag her feet and find herself having to implement an LEA scheme that she does not like at all.

2 Delegating the responsibility

A few days after the decision has been taken at the senior management meeting, Mrs Gatlin summons Mike Wade.

'I am glad to see that you are so positive about appraisal, Mike, because as school Staff Development Officer, I want you to take responsibility for its introduction. I have been very pleased with the way you have handled staff development so far. I know introducing appraisal will not be easy, so I should like you to give some thought to how we should proceed. Perhaps we could meet again next week, when you have had time to get some ideas together?'

Mike goes away and cogitates. He has only been in post for a year and a half and has found creating the whole apparatus of Inset a considerable challenge. Setting up the system was hard work, but he actually enjoyed it and felt that it was beginning to work well. He supports appraisal because he sees it as the logical culmination of the structure he is establishing, and feels that the teaching profession stands to gain from a system that provides teachers with a regular job review and discussion of their training needs. His main concern is the timing. He would prefer the existing system to run for two or three years before taking on appraisal as well. It has not been easy to gain acceptance for the Inset programme. Appraisal is even more sensitive; he knows that a number of staff will be hostile to the whole idea, so it is important that the climate is right for its introduction. Moreover, some staff might begin to think it is his fault that they are faced with one initiative on top of another. He still remembers, shortly after his promotion, a jealous member of staff accusing him of only being interested in getting yet another line onto his curriculum vitae. Mike can hardly tell Mrs Gatlin that although he supports appraisal he thinks the time is not ripe; he has been on the management team long enough to be aware that this is a period of major changes for education and that all the changes seem to be happening at the same time. His plans will have to take these problems into account.

3   Planning the process

Mike reviews the problem over the weekend and then drafts a working paper which he sends to the Head with a request that they meet to discuss it. He sees several stages to the introduction of appraisal and has set out a draft plan to show these stages. The ideas that follow come from his working paper.

4   Raising awareness

As with any major change, Mike feels that good preparation is essential. They cannot simply impose the new system and say 'Let's start appraisal next term.' Rather, they have to prepare the staff for appraisal. Because it is such a sensitive area this will take some time. First they need to raise awareness. The staff are not particularly well informed about appraisal so they need to be given information. Mike stresses the importance of involving the whole staff at this stage. He feels that trialling just one department could be counterproductive. There needs to be a lot of time for discussion. He argues that appraisal is more likely to succeed in the school if people are given the chance to air their fears, rather than feeling that their fears are ignored or swept under the carpet. An Inservice training day for the whole staff would, he feels, be the best way to begin the process. This, of course, could be supplemented by making available books, videos and other materials on appraisal.

5 Setting up the working party

Mike argues against going to the staff with a prearranged system.

'I do not think I should personally create a model even for discussion. I think we should set up a working party after the training day and they will do the next stage of planning. This will take a bit longer than if I do the work but it is more likely to gain acceptance from staff, as they may be less wary of a system they have created themselves than of one imposed by management. On the other hand, we must be careful that we do not produce the opposite effect of making the staff think we are leaving them to do all the work, so it might be a good idea for me to lead the working party. Obviously the group will have to be briefed very well about the current state of LEA thinking so that they do not come up with a scheme that will be unacceptable. It might be helpful and save us some time if I prepared some briefing papers as a starting point. As for the composition of the working party, I suggest that we use the same selection system that I have adopted for the Staff Development Committee, that is to ask for volunteers and then add any additional staff we need to balance the team.'

6 Designing the system

Mike considers that the working party would probably need most of the Autumn term to familiarise themselves with the information and design a system. He feels it would be a major mistake to rush things at this stage, as it is very important that the system should be one with which the staff will be comfortable. The working party will have to consider not just possible systems (the merits of hierarchical versus peer appraisal; what happens to large departments; whether there should be any element of choice in deciding your appraiser, etc) but also the mechanics of the system (how to fit in classroom observation and the appraisal interview; what the time structure should be; where to find sufficient interview space, etc).

'There are going to be a lot of problems to sort out, some of which will only emerge as we begin to talk through the issues.'

7 Training the personnel

Training for the staff who will act as appraisers is an essential part of preparation. They will need to learn listening and interviewing skills. Mike points out that some training will probably need to start before the structure is fully designed. He does not, however, see this as too much of a problem; all the indications from the pilot schemes are that appraisal is likely to have to be hierarchical, ie by one's line manager. If they begin to train a group of middle managers, they are likely to be targeting the right people. He probably needs to consult the county Adviser about organising the training, and would do that as soon as the basic procedure was agreed, as bookings often have to be made well in advance.

8 Trialling
Mike anticipates that by the Spring term they should be ready to test the system. The working party will probably have to decide precisely how this should be done, but the safest thing is either to use volunteers (though this might be rather haphazard) or persuade one or two departments to be guinea pigs. However it is organised, he feels that it is important for the scheme's credibility that the 'guinea pigs' include some members of the senior management team or the whole operation will be seen as just a 'top down' imposition.

9 Reviewing the system
After the trial run through there will need to be an assessment of how it went, with modifications made as necessary. This will mark the end of preparation and the structure will be ready to operate.

10 Implementation
Part of the working party's task will be to formulate a cycle of appraisal. Mike does not want to pre-empt their plans, but is prepared to argue that it will take at least a year to get appraisal going; he thinks it is highly unlikely that everyone will receive an appraisal in the first year. Indeed he feels that in the long run it would be better if the system came into operation gradually so that the school can cope with its demands in terms of time, training and rooms.

11 Head's reaction
Mrs Gatlin approves of Mike's draft scheme and of his method of tackling the problem. He has not disguised the potential problems nor provided all the answers, but he has shown a good understanding of the issues and has created a basic structure though

which they could work. She is pleased that he did not think he had to come up with a complete package immediately; she likes the emphasis he put on good preparation and is pleased that he wanted to involve staff in planning the appraisal that concerns them so closely. She also likes the kind of leadership he is prepared to offer the working party.

Case Study 11.3   *For action*
STRUCTURING AN APPRAISAL SYSTEM

Mike Wade set up a working party to plan an appraisal system for Bestwick Park High School. He hoped that they would be able to devise a system that followed the National Steering Group and DES regulations, while incorporating principles of good practice that the school considered to be important.

Mike gave the working party some documents which could be used to inform their thinking or to help them spark off ideas. Two examples of these are given below. Mike regarded it as essential to include some extracts from the report of the National Steering Group on Teacher Appraisal; he thought it would be pointless for the school to construct a system which was out-of-touch with what was happening nationally.

1 Criteria for an effective appraisal system

The people involved:
● want it
● understand it
● are commited to it
● are trained to participate in it
● keep it under review and develop it
● own it

The paperwork involved:
● is simple and not too time-consuming
● is realistic and job-related
● is open – in the sense that everyone knows what is involved
● is confidential between the appraiser and the appraisee

The system is used for:

- the self – development of the people involved
- counselling on people's needs
- analysing people's training needs
- helping with people's career development

R Kemp and M Nathan – *Middle Management in Schools* Blackwell 1989

2 The main components of the appraisal process

The working group understands appraisal not as a series of perfunctory periodic events, but as a continuous and systematic process intended to help individual teachers with their professional development and career planning, and to help ensure that the inservice training and deployment of teachers matches the complementary needs of the individual teachers and the school.

Drawing on the experience of the six pilot projects we recommend that the teacher appraisal programme has the following components:

- an initial meeting between the appraiser and the appraisee.
- self appraisal by the appraisee.
- classroom observation.
- collection of data from other sources agreed with the appraisee.
- an appraisal interview in which professional targets for action are agreed.
- the preparation of an appraisal statement, to be agreed by both parties.
- follow up including a formal review meeting.

National Steering Group *Report on School Teachers' Appraisal* 1989

Members of the working party submitted papers or memos on aspects of the system which would need special consideration.

Part of a paper from Vivienne Michael, Head of the Humanities Faculty

WHO SHOULD ACT AS APPRAISERS?

If appraisal is to be an integral part of the management of teachers, it is important that the appraiser should have the necessary authority to ensure that the appraisal is properly followed up. This makes it difficult to implement peer appraisal, because, although this has some advantages - it is the least threatening form of appraisal, and it can be both beneficial to discuss issues with a colleague who understands the situation well and helpful in improving classroom techniques - it has the major disadvantages that a colleague of the same rank will not have the knowledge of what is available nor the power to sort out the training and career development issues, or to provide practical solutions to problems that have emerged from the appraisal. Staff also need an occasional opportunity to talk through their own concerns with a senior member of staff and peer appraisal would not provide this.

The ACAS report has suggested that the appraiser of a teacher should be his or her immediate superior. In a secondary school this would mean that the heads of department or section would handle the appraisal of their team and that the Heads and Deputies would handle the appraisal of the middle managers. Some departments are very large and it is generally agreed that one person should not at any one time be involved in the appraisal of more than four people. To deal with this difficulty in the pilot schemes the appraiser has usually been someone with management responsibility for the appraisee, or, if that is not possible, the Head Teacher would have to nominate someone who is sufficiently experienced to ensure that the appraisal serves the needs of both the teacher and the school.

It is also recommended that no teacher - including the Head - is given any choice of who his/her appraiser should be, as it is thought that this would make it difficult to implement the system fairly and interfere with nominating the most appropriate person within the school's structure. This does not mean that requests for an alternative appraiser should never be considered. If there is a real conflict or dissatisfaction after trying to use the system, then clearly other arrangements should be made, but that should be a last resort.

Memo from Meriel Hemmings

WHAT SHOULD WE DO ABOUT THE DEPUTIES?

We have more or less agreed now about how our appraisal
system should work, but I feel that there is one area,
and a particularly sensitive one, which we haven't
addressed at all, and that we must sort it out before we
present our conclusions to the staff, ie. What do we do
about appraising the Deputy Heads?

A lot of thought has been given to how to organise the
Headteachers' appraisal. They are having a different
system from the rest of us, but none of the material that
Mike has given us dealt with how the Deputies should be
appraised. It is important that we get it right.

These are some of the issues that I think we must
consider:

*How much classroom appraisal is appropriate for
Deputies, as their responsibilities are predominantly
managerial?

*The conditions of service for Deputies are different
from other teaching staff. Should this be reflected in
the appraisal arrangements?

*Heads are to be appraised by two people - one person
with experience as a Head and one LEA Officer or Adviser.
Should the Head be the sole appraiser of the Deputies?

For action:
1   The material in the case study above could provide the basis
    for a group simulation – a working party meeting to design an
    appraisal system for Bestwick Park School.
2   You could use these documents as a working basis to try to
    design an appraisal system for your own school. (You may
    need to use Force Field Analysis, see page 57, to analyse the
    driving and resisting forces for change.)

Your role as a counsellor

Case Study 11.4   *For reflection*
RESOLVING CONFLICT: EVELYN CROFT

Yvonne Perkins, the Deputy Head, found Evelyn Croft waiting for her in her office when she returned from teaching the Third Form. Evelyn looked utterly fed up and rather weepy, so Mrs Perkins offered her a cup of coffee and probed gently to find out what was wrong.

I'm sorry to trouble you, but I didn't know who else to turn to. You have been here a long time and you may understand, though I don't suppose you can do anything to help. I know that I'm not up to date with some of the more recent innovations, but I don't approve of most of them especially empathy, and I prefer to give the children a thorough grounding in the facts of History. In the past my O Level and CSE results have always been good. Surely that's what really matters, not a lot of sideshows. Now apparently all my good work over the years counts for nothing. I'm considered an old fuddy duddy and parents write letters complaining about how I teach.

What really hurts me is that nobody bothered to talk to me about Mrs Dean's letter. They condemned me unheard. The Head must have sent Vivienne to watch my lesson, but she didn't tell me that there had been a complaint. Her visit made the children suspect that there was something wrong and I found it very offputting. 4E are difficult enough at the best of times. They are so easily distracted. Children these days seem unable to concentrate for more than a few minutes. Then when Vivienne left half way through my double lesson, the effect on the class was quite dreadful. I have never seen them behave as badly as they did yesterday. Mary Dean was one of the worst, of course. She is very plausible and looks absolutely angelic, but she's a real trouble maker.

I went to see Vivienne later to find out what was going on, and this is when I learnt that Mrs Dean had written in complaining about me. I had to ask Vivienne several times before I got to see a copy of the letter. She kept saying that it would only upset me, but for me it was worse not to know. Its main accusation was that I was old fashioned and the children found my lessons boring. I can live with that. After all it is only a matter of opinion, but I'm really upset about how I was treated. Why couldn't they have discussed the matter with me, not treated me like some sort of criminal on trial? It is Mary Dean who should be in trouble, not me. What's going to happen next? I am only trying to do my job in the best way that I can. I don't believe that playing silly games and pretending that it is work does the children any good at all. Now I feel totally humiliated by what has happened.

When Mrs Perkins saw Vivienne Michael later that day, it became clear that Vivienne's interpretation of events was very different from Evelyn's.

'There was a deputation from the Fourths a week or so ago. They are not being unreasonable. They know that they have to have some notes, but the problem is that Evelyn spends all the lessons dictating notes and what makes it worse is that the children have realised that she is still using her old O Level notes. She has not adjusted to GCSE at all, though it has now been in place for several years. I am not at all surprised that Mrs Dean has complained. I'm more surprised that it was not sooner and that she is the only one to do so. Mary is an able girl, a potential A Level student, and she is not being stretched at all in Evelyn's lessons. I'd be fed up in her position.'

When pressed about her visit to 4E's lesson, Vivienne said, 'Evelyn has resisted appraisal as she has resisted all other innovations. I regularly observe the lessons of other members of the Faculty. I could only stay for one period, not two, because I teach period 6 and had to go to my own lesson. Anyway she had been dictating notes for 40 minutes when I left. It is very difficult as she is not due to retire for four or five years yet, but she is totally set in her ways. Although I felt that the pupils were suffering, I put up with the situation because I felt that my attempts to get her to change would fail dismally and that my actions would only make matters worse, but now the pupils and their parents are beginning to complain and we can no longer ignore the situation.'

The situation as perceived by Evelyn Croft:
Mrs Croft's perception of the problem centred on her treatment by the Head and her Head of Faculty. She felt humiliated and that she had been treated 'as if she were a criminal, put on trial and condemned without being allowed to speak in her own defence'.

She will not admit that her teaching methods constitute a problem. She seems to believe that she is in the right and that it is her critics who are wrong. She is very resentful about Vivienne's visit to her classroom, and this is likely to be linked to the fact that she is actually sensitive about her teaching methods, and feels threatened by the possibility of appraisal. She is also frightened about what the possible outcome of the complaint might be; she wants to know what action the Head, who has not yet spoken directly to Evelyn, is likely to take. She has come to Yvonne Perkins because she hopes that Yvonne will be more sympathetic than Vivienne and might intercede with the Head on her behalf.

The situation as perceived by Vivienne Michael:
Vivienne's perception of the problem is centred on two connected issues – Mrs Croft's didactic teaching methods and her inflexible personality, which has made her resistant to change. Vivienne is also seeking to justify her own reluctance to address a problem of which she was fully aware, until she was forced into action by the pupils' behaviour and Mrs Dean's letter to the Head. She may also be worried that her tactics in handling the matter leave her open to criticism.

What is the role of the senior manager in this situation?
Dealing with conflict – a clash of personalities or ideas within a department – is an important part of a senior manager's role. Deputy Heads are frequently called upon to counsel and advise middle managers who are having difficulty managing members of their department, similarly teachers, who have a difference of opinion with their immediate manager, often look to the Deputy Head to provide a sympathetic ear.

In this kind of situation you have to counsel both sides, not just one, regardless of the fact that only one party may have directly sought your advice. Your task is not only to reconcile two individuals, but to resolve the conflict in the best interest of the school.

Resolving the problem

Initially Yvonne will probably have to counsel Evelyn and Vivienne separately, bringing them together later, after she has made some progress with them individually.

Yvonne will have start by dealing with Evelyn's hurt feelings. She needs to reassure her that she is a valued member of staff. She has to persuade Evelyn that the Head and her Head of Faculty are not simply picking on her and that no-one is deliberately seeking to humiliate her, before she can hope to succeed in getting her to address the sensitive area of her teaching methods. It may be a good idea for Yvonne to be present when Evelyn sees the Head. It is important for her peace of mind that Evelyn knows what Mrs Gatlin actually thinks and what effect the Head's reply to Mrs Dean's letter will have on her own position, but the interview is likely to be a difficult session for her and she may be less defensive if she has a sympathetic colleague present.

Vivienne's intentions may have been good, but her actions appear to have been disastrous. She needs to re-examine her whole approach to dealing with Evelyn as it is clearly not working. Avoiding the issue has meant that when it finally came into the open, it was more traumatic for everyone than if it had been confronted earlier. Now before Vivienne tries to convince Evelyn that there needs to be more variety in her teaching methods, Yvonne will have to counsel her about what strategies to adopt.

Procedures for classroom observation will need to be defined. As Head of Faculty, Vivienne is responsible for what is happening in Evelyn's classroom, so she was within her rights in visiting Mrs Croft's lesson, and Yvonne will have to make this clear to Evelyn, who is probably already suspects that the Head is likely to insist that Vivienne closely monitors 4E's progress. The insensitive way that Vivienne seems to have handled the whole episode, especially the observation of 4E's lesson, is another matter altogether. Classsroom observation should not have been a threatening experience for Mrs Croft and Yvonne may have to do some work with Vivienne in order to improve her approach.

Providing support for Evelyn

Evelyn's reliance on note-giving indicates not only her use of didactic methods, but also a holding operation. It suggests that Evelyn is dictating notes because she feels that otherwise she may lose control of what she considers to be a difficult class, so the problem of her relationship with 4E will also have to be explored.

It is important here that Vivienne does not take the easy way out and arrange a change of teacher for 4E; this will actually add to the problem as Evelyn will feel defeated by the pupils and rejected both by them and by her department. Yvonne will have to see 4E, particularly Mary Dean, who seems to have been the ringleader. Mary and her friends deserve good teaching, but this is no excuse for unruly behaviour, and this may also need to be made clear to Mrs Dean. Vivienne has given the impression that she supports the pupils against their teacher, who is a member of her department. Now if Evelyn is to be persuaded that she must review her teaching style, she must first be convinced that the school is supporting her in maintaining a good standard of discipline. Once this is in place, Evelyn is more likely to have the confidence to experiment with new techniques. Again she will need support which can be provided through Inset, team teaching, use of department workshops to prepare materials etc.

Using counselling techniques

In order to resolve a difficult situation Yvonne Perkins has had to use counselling techniques. Counselling involves talking with someone for a considerable length of time, possibly for a series of sessions, in a way which encourages him/her to talk, think through his/her problem or situation and find possible solutions.

These techniques include:

1 *Providing an opportunity for an individual to talk to you*
Not everyone will arrive at your office as Evelyn did. Sometimes you have to pick up vibes in the staffroom or you will notice that a member of staff looks upset or is performing less well than previously and you suspect something is wrong. Your job is to be sensitive to the need and provide an opportunity for the individual to talk to you or to the most appropriate person.

Counselling only works well in a private, unhurried and undisturbed setting. As a Deputy Head you can provide the privacy because you are likely to have an office of your own. Providing the time could be more of a problem for you. You will need about half an hour for a session to be effective, but as Deputy Head you are constantly interrupted by a flow of people coming to your office. To provide the necessary privacy you must put the engaged notice firmly on the door and not take phone calls.

Drawing people out

2   *Drawing people out – getting them to tell you what the*
problem is and how they feel about it

It was not difficult for Yvonne to get Evelyn to talk about her
problem as Evelyn had herself initiated the session. In other cases
you may have to encourage someone to start talking and then draw
them out. To do this you need to provide a relaxed setting. Sitting
at a 90° angle to the person or next to them, using easy chairs, can
help to get an interview started. Staying behind your desk reas-
serts your authority and could inhibit. Yvonne used the offer of
coffee to show Evelyn that she had time to spare and to encourage
her to start talking. To persuade someone to confide in you, you
will have to be both reassuring and non-threatening. Open ended
questions such as 'How do you feel about that?' also help to draw
someone out. You need to listen sympathetically, not interrupting
someone's flow once they have started. Making listening noises
such as 'mmmmmm', encourages, while not interrupting the person talking. If you regularly maintain eye contact and from time to
time briefly summarise what has been said it will reassure the
person that you are fully involved with what s/he is saying. Sometimes you will need to ask a concrete question in order to clarify a

point, but this will also show that you are seeking to understand, and you can then reassure, 'Yes, now I understand'.

3 *Helping them to think through the problem, by exploring the areas*

The next step is to help the person analyse the problem by establishing what the main areas or issues are. In Evelyn's case the areas included:

● the complaint made against her by a parent
● her teaching methods
● her relationship with 4E
● appraisal/classroom observation

4 *Exploring possible solutions in order to arrive at the most satisfactory outcome for the person involved*

With both Evelyn and Vivienne, Yvonne had to explore the possible consequences of their actions. In this case the outcomes could include:

● a deterioration in relationships because each blames the other for what has occurred
● Evelyn refuses to change her ways and takes early retirement
● The Head reprimands Evelyn/Vivienne or both teachers
● Evelyn is taken off this teaching group
● Mary Dean is transferred to another History set
● Mary Dean is put on report
● The progress of 4E is monitored over a period of half a term
● Evelyn Croft agrees to review her teaching style
● Support and Inset is provided for Evelyn
● Vivienne is sent on a management course with special emphasis on staff development and counselling.

The aim in counselling is for the person to arrive at their own solution. The role of the counsellor is to help and encourage, and to support any solution which emerges from the session, but in this case several people were involved and the solution would have to be acceptable to the Head. For this reason you are likely to find that in dealing with conflict involving staff, pupils and parents your role goes beyond that of a counsellor and you have to manage the situation as well as advise the individuals.

5   *Providing continued support*

At the end of the first phase of counselling, hopefully some form of action plan will have been agreed. For Vivienne and Evelyn this would clarify what is expected of each of them and what period of time would be involved. It is likely that some continued support of either or both parties will be needed. Yvonne should try to make it low key, unobtrusive, but readily available when required.

Case Study 11.5   *For discussion*
SOME SITUATIONS

1   Annabel

Yvonne Perkins had noticed that Annabel Miles was looking rather 'under the weather' and when she heard her snap at a colleague in the staffroom, she looked for an opportunity to invite her for a chat. At first Annabel was reluctant to talk, she said that she didn't want to make trouble for anybody. When however, Mrs Perkins reassured her and offered help, a much relieved Annabel talked freely.

Annabel (MPG with allowance A) is a year tutor to a lively group of Fourth Year pupils. She also has special responsibility for visits and exchanges in the Modern Languages Department. She is scheduled to arrange a school exchange with a school in Bordeaux at half term. In addition to teaching, preparing and marking for her language classes, she co-ordinates the Third Year netball team. She has been asked to do some extra coaching in the coming weeks as the team is involved in a borough inter-schools tournament. It is also coming up to half year reports. As well as writing eight sets of reports herself, she has to collate her tutor group's reports and to complete 30 tutor comments, including special reports on two girls who are persistently truanting.

Annabel has a beautiful singing voice and has hitherto been a keen member of the local operatic society, but now she is seriously thinking of dropping out of the next production because she is finding her work load so heavy. Under pressure from her Head of Department Roger Russell, from her Head of Year, Nigel North and from the Head of Girls' PE, Gina Pollins, she feels pulled in too many directions.

I wouldn't have come to you, because it felt like telling tales, but I'm actually glad you made me talk because I am at my wits' end to know what to do. They are all asking for my efforts at the same time, none of them seems to understand the pressure I am under from the other two. I don't want my teaching standard to fall, and I don't want to skimp any of the extra tasks I have been given. Please Mrs Perkins, whose tasks should take priority?

You are Yvonne Perkins. Discuss what you will do to help Annabel.

2   Vera and Fiona

Vera Southern, Second in the English Department has come to Yvonne Perkins for help.

... I always assumed that I would inherit the department when old Cheasley finally retired. After all I had been running it for him for over three years. I knew it would be difficult after Mrs Gatlin came and began to make changes, but I felt that I was rising to meet the challenge and that I was making a success of things. I enjoyed all the organising and found that I was coping easily with the demands of running a department and that I was actually reading quite a lot. Then when the job came up, there were a lot of outside candidates and it was very competitive and I made a complete hash of the interview. I froze up and could not think of anything to say. When I didn't get the post I felt that I had lost status in the staffroom. I know that a lot of people were quite pleased to see me fail and that hurt a lot. Now I am finding it really difficult to adjust to the new situation. I have got used to having a lot of responsibility. I obviously can't talk to my new Head of Department about this, but I need advice urgently and you helped me a lot when I first came to the school.

Fiona Bruce, the new Head of English also sought Mrs Perkins' advice.

I heard that Vera wanted the post very badly and had expected to get it, so I wasn't too worried when she wasn't very welcoming when I first arrived. I thought this was a situation that I was mature enough to cope with, and that if I treated her reasonably, we would both be professional enough to ride it out. After all it happens often enough.

But after two terms it hasn't improved at all and in fact at times it has been very difficult indeed. She has an extremely sharp tongue and cannot resist sniping at me, particularly at department meetings, where she not only belittles everything that I suggest, but regularly tries to create the impression that perfectly normal procedures are new and quite unreasonable demands upon my team. Sometimes this means that it is very difficult for me to get them to co-operate. It is very divisive and is having a bad effect upon department morale . . .

How should Yvonne go about resolving the conflict between Vera and Fiona?

12 Managing the whole curriculum

What is the whole curriculum?

The Education Reform Act of 1988 (ERA) has had significant effects upon the management of schools:

- It strengthened the role of central government
- It limited the role of LEAs
- It gave more autonomy to schools
- It made schools more responsible to parents and the public
- It created the framework of the National Curriculum

As a result those involved in running the nation's schools changed from being the administrators of LEA policies to being the managers of institutions, with far more powers – particularly over finance and resources – than they had ever had in the past. In real terms, however, this increased autonomy was limited by the creation of a curricular framework – the National Curriculum. Moreover the National Curriculum alone was not seen as providing the necessary breadth of education, so the Act instructed schools to deliver what has become known as the Whole Curriculum.

Schools were given

The statutory responsibility to provide a broad and balanced curriculum which:

- *Promotes the spiritual, moral, cultural, mental and physical development of pupils.*
- *Prepares pupils for the opportunities, responsibilities and experiences of adult life.*

The quotation above comes from *Curriculum Guidance 3 – The Whole Curriculum* published by the National Curriculum Council. The information provided in that document is used throughout this chapter.

In terms of what should be taught, the introduction of the National Curriculum has prescribed ten core and foundation subjects plus RE, to be studied until the age of 14, after which more flexibility is allowed. The National Curriculum core subjects are: English, Mathematics, Science; the foundation subjects are Technology, History, Geography, a Modern Foreign Language, Art, Music and Physical Education.

A balanced whole curriculum is expected to furnish opportunities for the study of additional subjects which will 'extend knowledge, interests and skills'. Finally, cross-curricular elements have to be integrated into the curriculum. They are the ingredients which 'tie together the broad education of the individual' and augment the basic curriculum provided by the core and foundation subjects.

The NCC has identified three aspects in the cross-curricular elements:

- Core skills – eg communications, problem solving or IT
- Dimensions – eg equal opportunities
- Five themes – Economic and Industrial understanding
  Careers Education and Guidance
  Education for Citizenship
  Environmental Education
  Health Education

Although the National Curriculum has not yet reached the Sixth Form, 16–19 Education is also being broadened to include core skills such as communications, problem solving and numeracy. This move to increase the breadth and width of their studies is being described as providing Sixth Form pupils with their 'Entitlement Curriculum'.

What does whole curriculum planning involve?

The most immediate effect of ERA is that a school's main priority has become the delivery of the whole curriculum and its resources are having to be deployed to ensure its implementation. Whilst it is possible that implementing the changes demanded by the National Curriculum and the 16–19 reforms will cause your school no trouble at all, because the necessary elements are almost in place already, for most schools major curriculum change will be necessary and will have to be planned for and implemented over a period of years.

Other changes introduced by ERA, particularly LMS, are also making their impact on schools and the challenge for the school's senior management team is considerable. The school will have to find strategies for:

- Enhancing the achievement of pupils
- Improving the effectiveness of the school
- Managing development and change

This has affected how the planning of the curriculum is approached. The various aspects of planning have to be integrated in the interests of effectiveness. This necessitates the production of a corporate Management Development Plan embracing all aspects of policy and development. This DEVELOPMENT PLAN is becoming the school's main planning vehicle, required by the LEA as a three or five year plan with annual updates. Because of the importance placed on the delivery of the Whole Curriculum, in many respects this plan is curriculum led, but it is much more complex than a curriculum development plan, relating the curriculum policy to the school's overall aims and taking fully into account all the resource implications of the policies to be adopted.

By far the best source of guidance for constructing a corporate development plan is to be found in *Planning for School Development, Advice to Governors, Headteachers and Teachers* by David Hargreaves, David Hoskins, Marilyn Leask, Joe Connolly and Paul Robinson (DES 1989). The ideas, advice and terminology employed in that booklet are used throughout this chapter.

Constructing a school's Management Development Plan is such

a large task that it is clearly too onerous to become the responsibility of one individual. In most schools it is perceived as a corporate responsibility undertaken by the senior management team. The school's curriculum manager may take a leading role, but the overall task is likely to be divided up into a number of smaller, more manageable tasks, with different members of the team taking responsibility for different areas. This is having an effect on the senior management team itself; it emphasises its importance to the effective management of the school and makes it vital that it fulfils its function as a team.

Processes in development planning

There are four stages or processes in development planning:

---

1   *Audit* – a school reviews its strengths and weaknesses.
2   *Plan Construction* – priorities for development are selected and turned into specific targets.
3   *Implementation* – of the priorities and targets.
4   *Evaluation* – the success in implementation is checked.

From: *Planning for School Development* Hargreaves, Hoskins, Leask, Connolly and Robinson (DES 1989)

---

1   Conducting a curriculum audit

The purpose of the audit
The audit is a review of current provision to assess its strengths and weaknesses and to see how far it matches with ERA requirements. It is asking the question 'Where are we now?'

It is also a means of collecting the data needed for the development plan, and will provide a basis for selecting priorities during the construction of the plan.

It has one other purpose: carrying out this kind of review aims to help to raise staff awareness of what is happening in the school. Departments tend to be immersed in their own area of activity; participating in the curriculum audit should help staff gain a more holistic view of how the school operates.

What kind of data will be analysed in the audit?

1 *The aims and values of the school* The aims describe the fundamental purpose and direction of the school, so they serve as important criteria by which the school assesses itself. The audit will ask the question 'How far are these aims being achieved in practice?'

2 *Information about subjects* Subject departments may each need to do an individual audit and indicate what development is needed over the period in question.

3 *Cross-curricular elements* A mapping exercise may need to be carried out to check the provision of the cross-curricular elements. This exercise will help show where the overlap is and what gaps there are. Some information will also be needed about the availability of extra-curricular activities.

4 *Teaching methods* Another mapping exercise will be needed to analyse the range of teaching and learning strategies being used in the school.

5 *Information* will be needed about methods of assessment and recording procedures.

6 *Resources* Information will be needed about how and why the school used its resources during the previous year, whether existing resources match needs and how resource needs are currently determined.

7 *Whole school policies* You will need to check whether whole school policies exist on all the current issues, whether they complement or contradict each other, how they match with the school's aims, and if they will need revision to bring them into line with national and local guidelines. You must also check to see whether they are actually being implemented.

8 *Curriculum policy* Data will be needed about the way that decisions have been taken in the past about how the curriculum is organised and its expression in the school's timetable.

How should the audit be carried out?

The list above was not intended to be comprehensive, rather it shows some of the aspects which could be considered. This audit can vary in scope. Some schools might undertake a full-scale review of their life and work; most will prefer to focus on specific areas each year and build up the review over several years. Even so, collecting this kind of data means a lot of work. Decisions will need to be taken about which areas to select and how to collect, collate and analyse the relevant information so that it is of good quality but involves the minimum expenditure of time and effort. As a senior manager you are likely to be given the responsibility for co-ordinating the audit and for producing the overview, ie the summary and the list of issues or recommendations for the development plan, but the task of undertaking the audit will need to be broken down into a number of smaller tasks and carried out by groups of staff. This serves two purposes – it means that no one person takes on too much work and it involves a lot of the staff. Inset time could be allocated for this, either on one of the Inservice days or through the general school Inset programme.

2   Constructing the development plan

Constructing the development plan is a task that is likely to be given to one of the senior management team. Although it will use the same structure as a development plan for an individual initiative, it is a much more complex document, so how do you carry out this task effectively?

The more carefully the plan is constructed, the easier it will be to implement. The development plan is intended to be a working document that is easily updateable as the educational goalposts change. The plan should be realistic and within the capability of the school to implement.

Not all the challenges facing schools can be responded to immediately; the main task of the construction phase is to decide which issues should become priorities for the first year of the plan and which developments will have to happen in subsequent years.

How do you set about determining priorities? Determining priorities means making decisions about: which issues are more *important* or more *urgent* than others; how to place the issues in a sequence over time.

Among the range of techniques for evaluating possible choices, two seem to offer themselves as having potential for schools:

1   *Cost Benefit Analysis* – This seeks to analyse the benefits which might accrue from the possible sources of action and assess them against the cost required to achieve these benefits. This may be direct physical cost or it may be opportunity cost.

2   *Scenario planning* – This involves 'developing a vision of success', ie trying to paint a picture of what might happen if the

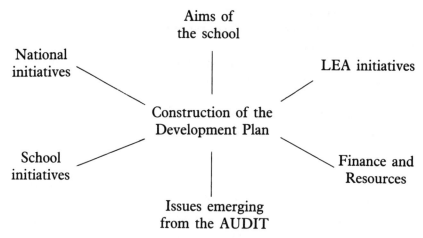

Figure 9   *Factors affecting construction of the development plan*

chosen course of action was pursued. What would the end result look like? Would the scene then carry credibility? If this technique is used some contingency planning might need to be built into the planning, as some of the steps of the development might lead in different directions from the original senario.

Who should decide priorities?
This kind of job is usually done best by a task group or working party. This may be the senior staff constituting itself as a working party for this purpose, but you may prefer to include a representative selection of staff on the team that makes the first selection and then refer the draft to the senior management team. In some schools there will a curriculum sub-committee including both governors and staff whose brief will include undertaking this work.

The final selection of priorities will need to take into account both the school's own interests and national and local priorities, and it will have to be approved by the school's governing body. Figure 9 examines factors affecting construction of the development plan.

The content of the plan
The development plan is likely to be about four or five pages in length and include:

- the context of development
- long, medium and short-term targets
- the justification of the targets
- resource requirements – this should include teachers, ancillary staff, time, materials and accommodation
- staff training needs
- allocation of responsibilities
- methods of monitoring and evaluation

Recording the decisions

Your school development plan may be a lengthy and complex document, from which it is difficult to pick out the main developments. A useful way to record and highlight planning decisions is to use an action plan proforma (see Figure 10). You can use this in two ways:

1   To sum up a particular section, eg to list curriculum decisions.
2   As the final section of the plan, providing a summary of the actions to be taken and indicating who is responsible and what the time scale is to be.

Using the proforma will also help you evaluate the plan, as the last column provides a brief record of the outcome of each action.

3   Implementing the development plan

It is easier to construct a development plan than to make it work. Successful implementation needs both pressure and continual support, and it is a key responsibility of the senior management team to provide this.

Making the plan work involves

1   *Motivation-boosting to sustain commitment*
- Show *interest* in the progress of the development. It is difficult for even the most commited teacher to sustain enthusiasm when an initiative hits difficulties just at the time when s/he is really hard pressed with reports, marking and endless meetings. Fairly regular general inquiries about how things are going demonstrates to a hard-pressed teacher that all his/her hard work has at least been noticed and valued.

		ACTION	TIME REQUIRED	DEADLINE	RESPONSIBILITY OF?	CONSULTATION WITH?	OUTCOME
Marketing	1.	Revise School Prospectus	6 months	June – ready for next intake	Marketing Committee	Headteacher and Governors	
	2.	Improve liaison with feeder Schools	Ongoing		Head of First Years	Deputy Head – Pastoral Marketing Committee	
	3.	Improve liaison with industry	Ongoing		Deputy Head	Work Experience Co-ordinator relevant HoDs.	
Curriculum	1.	Introduce Technology GCSE	9–10 months	By next Sept.	Technology Co-ordinator	Deputy Head Curriculum Governors' Curriculum Committee	
	2.	Introduce Balanced Science	8 months	By next Sept.	Head of Science	Deputy Head Curriculum Governors' Curriculum Committee	

Figure 10 *An Action Plan proforma*

- Some *praise* for what has been achieved will always be appreciated.
- Set aside a regular session with the team leaders. Staff may not come and consult you unless you set aside a regular time for this to happen. It will keep you informed of progress and it also provides an informal opportunity for you to find out about any problems.
- Go and see the development in action from time to time, so that, for example, you know what implementing language diversification entails. This will also be appreciated. Remember to tell them that you are coming – don't just turn up, as this might be seen as a threat.
- Attend team meetings occasionally. This is often helpful for the team, particularly if it is a planning session where you will be able to advise on the feasibility of different schemes.
- Provide ample staff development and support it. Curriculum development usually needs staff development as well. It is always counterproductive to skimp on Inset.

2   *Checking the progress of implementation*
This involves monitoring the developments at regular intervals and providing help where needed. Progress checks provide an interlude in which you can take stock and creative thinking can be applied to setbacks or difficulties. Problems that could emerge may include

- Difficulties in keeping to the original timescale
- Obstacles or contingencies that have not been allowed for in the original plan
- Need to modify the course content

There are a whole variety of ways in which you can provide support, eg

- Restructure the team to strengthen it
- Modify the timetable to provide time to slow the pace
- Extend some targets over a longer period of time
- Bring in an Adviser or Advisory Teacher to act as consultant
- Re-assign roles and responsibilities within the existing team
- Provide Inset time

4 Evaluating the plan

Implementing and evaluating the plan are inter-related. The progress check described in the previous section was part of the formative evaluation process and provided information that you needed in order to improve the programme of development. It actually contributes to the process of development. There is also no single point on the school's calendar that is exclusively concerned with evaluation, as different initiatives will come into operation at different times dependent upon where they are on the priority list. Evaluation is concerned with assessing the success of the plan and helping the school to take stock of what has been achieved.

Evaluation procedures have been fully dealt with in Chapter 9, but in terms of managing the whole curriculum and evaluating the management plan, what you are likely to have to do is report back annually on the experience of the plan during the year.

This will involve you in reviewing how far individual targets have been met; estimating what changes of practice there have been as a result of the plan; assessing the extent to which the school's aims have been furthered, and assessing the impact of the plan on the pupils' learning and achievement.

This review will contribute to the next year's mini-audit and thus itself form part of the next planning cycle. Many LEAs now insist that the school Management Plan is discussed annually with the school's Attached Adviser and this forms part of the evaluation process.

Case Study 12.1 *For reflection*
THE MANAGEMENT CYCLE

The chart shows a school's yearly management cycle and clearly
illustrates the central role played by development planning in
managing a school under ERA.

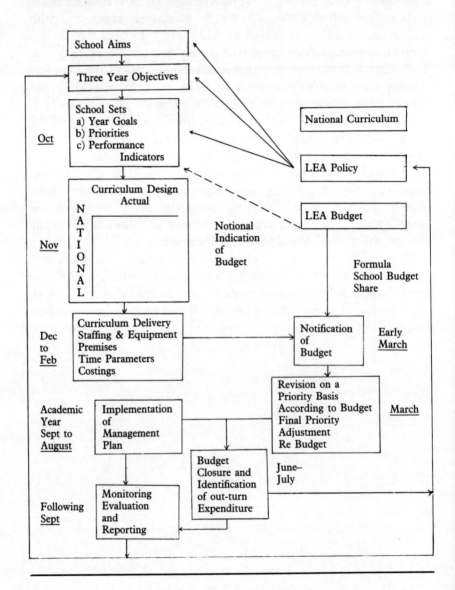

13 Managing resources

Local Management of Schools has given over to the school the management of its budget. The school does not determine the budget, that is done by the LEA through its budget formula arrangements, but the school has to decide how to deploy the funding that it receives and it can try to supplement it by generating additional income. Some LEAs are phasing in the change over a period of time in order to ease schools into the new system, others have immediately entered full formula funding. There are considerable benefits to a school and its pupils in having control of its own budget, providing that the amount in the budget is sufficient to service the school's needs. You are able to vire between budget headings, that is you can move the money about from one budget heading to another eg from equipment to staffing, which you could not do in the past. You can also carry money over from one year to another so that you can build up funds for a major development. For the senior manager LMS means increased responsibilities, because the Head is likely to delegate much of the detailed work of managing the finances to one or more of the senior management team.

Resources Manager, Finance Manager, LMS Manager – these are some of the titles you might have if you have been given the task of co-ordinating the school's financial planning. What will your role entail?

You may have to undertake all the functions associated with the management of finance and resources or the task may be broken up and shared between two or more of the team. It will involve you in some or all of the following activities:

- Finding out what the school's resources are and assessing how they can be used effectively
- Constructing the school's financial plan or budget
- Controlling the budget
- Managing the budget information system
- Managing the ancillary staff eg the bursar, or whoever does the ordering, and the office staff who input the data into the computer.

Auditing the resources

An important first task for you as Resources Manager is to carry out an audit of the school's resources. The purpose of the audit is to ensure an appropriate match between the school's development plan and the available resources. The collection of information about resources forms part of the overall audit carried out before constructing the school management plan: this has been described in Chapter 12 (Managing the Whole Curriculum).

What are the main issues that you should address?

1 What are the school's resources – human, material and financial?
2 How has the school deployed its resources in the previous year?
3 Why did the school deploy its resources in this way?
4 Were there any control mechanisms?
5 Were there any arrangements for judging whether the resources had been used effectively?

Your investigation of the resources will involve you in analysing:

- the rationale for the deployment of teaching staff
- the ways in which the support staff were used
- the previous year's expenditure on consumables and equipment
- the running costs, eg heating, lighting, telephone bills etc
- how the accommodation was allocated and used
- what the sources of income were, how much the school had generated for itself and what was the potential to increase it

This list is not meant to be comprehensive. You can probably add many more aspect of resource management.

Creating the budget

The budget is the school's financial plan and its preparation and control is an integral part of the process of management.

Some approaches to constructing a budget:

1   What is the minimum on which the school can manage?

If you have been given a budget well below what you have received in the past, this may be the approach that you will have to use. You are trying to work out what is the absolute minimum on which the school can still keep going. There will come a point below which it is impossible to run the school, eg you cannot keep going on only two teachers.

2   What do I have to do to keep things as they are?

This means using last year's budget as your basis and assuming that costs will stay the same. This is the most popular and least threatening approach for inexperienced resource managers, who are not used to dealing with a detailed budget and to whom managing income from a variety of sources will be new. It is the least radical approach because it enables things to continue as they have always been. This approach is called managing a Stand Still Budget. A variation on this which gives some more scope, is an Incremental Budget. This means that you still derive next year's budget by reference to this year's budget, and perhaps you make some minor variations, but you leave the general pattern of expenditure untouched.

3   How do I budget for development?

Budgeting for development means that you start by deciding what you want to achieve. This form of budget is objective led, not resource led, education led and not budget led. Each proposed activity has to justify its place in the budget each year. It will not continue to be undertaken simply because it was there the previous year. This approach is known as zero-based budgeting or output budgeting because it requires the budget to be built up from scratch every year. This kind of budget is the most radical and adventurous, but it has many advantages. It allows you to plan ahead over a period of time and forces you to take decisions about priorities.

Your plans are likely to add up to more than the your total delegated budget, so you won't be able to afford everything that you want to do. You will have to prioritise. To do this you will have to take into account your fixed costs, ie the costs such as providing premises, facilities and essential staff irrespective of the numbers of pupils in the school. You will also have to make sure that money 'ear-marked' for particular activities does not become merged into the overall sum. Inset funding, for example, is delegated to the school through the LEATGS arrangements, but you cannot vire it and it can only be spent on Inset. Once you have removed this 'slice' of funding, you will have to decide which are the developments to which you are irrevocably committed and which you consider to be less essential this year and how they would fit over a two or three year scale. What does not work is to try to chop 5% or 10% off the estimates for all the proposals in order to fit them to the amount of money available! To succeed, a development has to be adequately supported, so it is wiser not to start a project this year if you cannot give it the resourcing that it needs.

Your computer information system may help you decide priorities, because with it you could set up a spreadsheet to project the costs of alternative ways of achieving your desired objectives, so that you can identify the cheapest methods.

Figure 11 is an example of a specimen budget for a primary and a secondary school. Exemplars of this kind were produced by LEAs to help schools become familiar with the main budget headings and gain some idea of what sums were likely to be involved. For historic reasons it was difficult for LEAs to provide school managers with a precise schedule of costs, and many items had to be imputed. This is one of the reasons why close monitoring of the budget is essential for the first few years.

Controlling the budget

You will need to monitor the budget closely to ensure month by month that spending in each budget category stays in line with the plan.

	Primary school (£)	Secondary school (£)
Employees:		
Teachers	131,150	1,110,174
Clerical and support staff	7,874	58,796
Manual staff	18,275	50,183
Premises:		
Maintenance	28,633	85,974
Energy costs	2,586	36,289
Rent and rates	8,426	61,342
Other	1,650	5,169
Supplies and services:		
General equipment	2,953	40,932
Educational equipment	4,303	60,437
Other	7,000	30,000
Total expenditure	212,850	1,529,296
Less income:		
Sales, fees and charges	80	5,146
Donations and other income	7	984
Total income	87	6,130
Net expenditure	212,763	1,523,166

From B Fidler and G Bowles – *Effective Local Management of Schools* Longman, 1989

Figure 11   *Indicative budgets for a primary and a secondary school*

Checking is likely to reveal that you have over or underspent in one or more of the areas, ie even if the total estimated and actual budgets match exactly, you may find variations in the individual budget headings.

If the actual expenditure proves to be out of step with the estimate for the particular category, what should you do:

- take no action because you believe that it will correct itself next month.
- work out corrective action eg either money will need to be moved in or out of that area by a process of virement, or you will have to work out how to bring the budget back on course later on in the year.
- use the contingency fund to balance the books?

Your responsibilities are likely to include producing a Budgetary Control Report. This should indicate:

1 Actual expenditure to date.
2 Expected expenditure for the year.
3 Variance between the two totals.
4 Adjustments to the overall plan.

Evaluating the budget

At the end of a budgetary cycle you will need to evaluate it. This involves:

1 Assessing how the money has been spent
2 Relating outcomes to objectives
3 Deciding whether it has all been worthwhile ie cost effective.

A budgetary system should:
- respond equitably to the needs of different subject areas
- enable priorities to be taken into account
- promote organisational objectives
- encourage innovation
- facilitate long-term planning
- be easily understood
- be widely accepted within the organisation.

T Simkins and D Lancaster *Budgeting and Resource Allocation in Educational Institutions* Sheffield City Polytechnic, 1987

Income generation

Generating income for the school may be one of your responsibilities if you have become the school's Resources Manager. There has been a lot of debate about the principle of teachers spending time fundraising for the school. If you have to deal with this issue you should be aware of and understand the arguments.

The case against fund raising
- It is the responsibility of the government to provide adequate funding for state education.
- It distracts teachers from their primary task of educating pupils.
- Teachers lack the appropriate skills – if they had wanted to be entrepreneurs they would have gone into business, not teaching.
- If we do it now it will become expected of us and another burden will be permanently placed upon schools.

The case for generating income
- Income generation is a means of securing educational ends, not an end in itself.
- The LMS formula funding system, tied to age-weighted pupil numbers and to average rather than actual teacher costs, simply does not provide enough money for a school to be pro-active.
- If the school does not supplement its income with some fundraising, it will not be able to provide some important activities.
- If the school cannot offer as attractive a programme as its competitors, this could affect pupil recruitment.

Because the issue has been controversial, it is essential that you handle it with sensitivity. It is also an area where you really cannot force unwilling staff to participate, so if you are asked to undertake responsibility for managing fundraising, you will need to give some thought to the most appropriate way of approaching the task.

How do you go about the task of generating income?

You don't have to do it all yourself!

The fact that you have become the school's Resources Manager does not mean that you have personally to be its principal fundraiser. It is unlikely to be cost effective for any school to use a large part of the time of a senior teacher or a deputy head in this way. Your task as the manager is to come up with suggestions as to how the school should tackle the problem, not to try to do it all personally.

Who should be the fundraisers?

There are a variety of ways that a school can approach selecting a fundraiser, the suggestions here are just some examples:

- Appoint a fundraiser – finance it from the school's LMS budget instead of a member of the teaching staff.
- Set up a Fundraising Committee composed of governors, the PTA or the staff or any combination, ie whatever is most appropriate for your school.
- Advertise in the local paper for a part-timer ie for one or two days a week. This could suit someone who had recently retired.
- Persuade industry to let you use one of their managers or one of their graduate recruits to draw up a list of suggestions.
- Seek a volunteer from amongst the parents.

Notice that you may want someone just to get you going or on a very part-time basis. The task for this person or group would be to generate ideas and to work out how to put them into operation.

What are the main issues to consider?

1 *What are we doing now?*

Most schools are already involved in some fundraising activities. These will need to be reviewed. Three tests will show you how good these functions are:

- Are they attracting much support?
- Are they taking up a lot of time?
- Are they bringing in much income?

If you have been running a Summer Fayre for the last 12 years, but it has been harder and harder to get staff, pupils and parents to contribute to it or support it, and the income from it is declining, perhaps you should drop it for a bit and try something else this year.

The vital question is, are you having to spend a lot of time and work hard on an event to raise a small amount of money? If this is the case you need to rethink the whole fundraising programme.

2 *Can we save money for the school by economising?*

Making economies tends to be a short-term solution and never wins you friends. It is not unreasonable for staff to expect good working conditions and proper resourcing for all the new initiatives that they have to deliver, but spending some money in order that the running costs for the building are kept low could be cost effective and leave more money for educational items such as textbooks. This approach involves such things as an energy survey of the school – you can probably get a local firm to do this for you. What it does not mean is that you have to spend all your time getting staff and pupils to turn off the lights.

3 *What can we do to get more out of the present system?*

When you review the activities that you are already engaged in, it will probably spark off some thoughts about how you could expand them or use them more effectively. Better publicity or a change in the timing of an existing function might attract more support for it. Giving a new emphasis to the annual sale could give it a whole new lease of life.

4 *What new activities or ideas can we generate?*

One of the tasks of the fundraising group will be to brainstorm new projects with which the school could become associated in order to increase its revenue. A number of people working together are usually more creative than a single person working alone.

Some ideas that a fundraising committee would want to consider

The suggestions listed below cover the general range of fundraising activities currently in vogue and their purpose is to provide a variety of ideas (a bank of suggestions) from which you can develop specific plans.

1 *Lettings* – deriving income from letting the school premises or its sports facilities. Remember here to take into account wear and tear, heating and lighting costs when estimating the advantages or disadvantages of a particular let. One good let may pay you better than constant small lets and be less work overall for your caretaker.

2 *Sales* – usually handled by the PTA. Termly jumble sales have long been a feature of school fundraising. Car boot sales are also popular and can provide a regular input to school funds. Xmas or Summer Fayres raise larger amounts, but need more work and a lot more planning than jumble sales. Franchising out stalls to craft fairs suits some school better than running the fair itself. Within a franchised event you may still be able to sell refreshments and make members for the PTA.

3 *Functions* Fashion shows, Xmas or Summer balls, Square, Scottish or Country and Western dances, Discos etc are just some of the examples of functions that schools hold. The success of this type of function often depends on whether you have matched the function to its target group appropriately, and how good your planning and publicity is.

4 *Events* Productions such as the school play or concert or evenings on a particular theme should aim not only to display the school to advantage, but to generate some income as well.

5 *Donations* Covenants are becoming an important source of income for schools and it could be an idea for the committee to undertake a covenanting drive while the law still permits it. NB When was the last time you put up the amount you get from school fund and dare you risk asking for more? Circulating old pupils can sometimes prove a profitable exercise for the school in terms of generating income.

6 *Advertising* eg allowing a bank to call itself the school bank could bring in some much needed income. Selling advertising space in the school magazine or display space round the school are also ways of earning income through advertising. Each school will need to decide what it consider appropriate to its own philosophy and ethos.

7 *Sponsorship* This means attracting help from local or national industry. Usually you need a parent or personal contact in

order to establish the initial link with the firm. You are likely to find that industry is generous with sponsorship in kind (eg computing equipment that they have finished with but could serve you for several years and which would cost you a lot of money to buy), as long as it is not deluged with too many requests. Industrial training or placements could provide a valuable opportunity for your staff and work experience opportunities could be forthcoming for your pupils. Do not forget the real value of these items. It is totally unrealistic, however, for you to expect large handouts of ready money – most companies do not have it to give and there is no reason why they should give you handouts. It is much more educationally valid as well as effective to focus your requests upon particular projects than to make a general or unspecific plea for money; it needs to be clear to the company what the gift is to be used for.

14 Promoting the school

Marketing Manager is a title that has begun to appear in a senior manager's job description. If the Head has called you to her office and told you that she wants you to undertake responsibility for marketing as well as the 10001 other functions that you have already, what precisely does it entail?

Marketing is about presenting the school to its public, that is its potential clients, ie its prospective parents, the parents of pupils already in the school, and the general public such as local residents and employers with whom the school and its pupils have dealings. It is also about reacting to the impressions that the public may already have. Marketing has the connotation of being 'offensive' ie very aggressive; you cast doubts on the quality of education available at your competitor's school and use any means to try to divert pupils to your school. This is *not* what good marketing is about and is likely sooner or later to rebound on the school that resorts to using it. Marketing is more than 'selling the school'. Responsive marketing is concerned with achieving a balance between what the 'customer' wants and the needs and aims of the organisation.

There are two main reasons why a school needs to market itself:

1 *To attract more pupils* Open enrolment and the fact that the LMS funding formula is largely based on age-weighted pupil numbers has meant that schools have had to try to attract more pupils in order to maintain or increase their roll. This has meant either competing against other local schools in the state system or with nearby independent schools.

2   *To improve the image of your school*   Your school will have
made an impression in the minds of the local people, who read
about the exploits of your pupils in the local press and see your
pupils in the shops and on the buses. A lot of information is
being given out through the media concerning education. How
far this information is understood will vary enormously and
there is a need to educate the public about the quality of what
schools are providing. In the past schools did not worry much
about their image. Notifications to parents, for example, were
likely to be very poorly presented. Now, not just because we
are in a competitive environment, the school has to improve
the way that it presents itself.

Explaining to your colleagues that failing to attract sufficient
pupils can lead to staff cuts or even closure, and that if they want
all that expensive equipment, they will need to find a sponsor to
provide it for them, could easily make you the most unpopular
member of the senior management team, so how do you approach
the task of marketing the school?

How to market the school

1   Convince your colleagues

A lot of teachers feel very strongly that marketing is not
what they are there to do and that it detracts from their primary
task, which is to teach their subject to children. Reading about
schools who have turned themselves into companies to market
goods or services has reinforced their initial feelings of hostility to
the whole idea. They feel threatened by it because it is so alien to
the ethos of schools in the past and they question whether it is
a proper use of teachers' or pupils' time. So if you are asked to
become the school's Marketing Manager, you will not only be
trying to promote the school, you will also have to convince some
of your colleagues that what you are doing is worthwhile.

The financial argument may be unpalatable to some teachers,
but it is important that they do understand it. To make it convincing, you should not be the only person from the senior management team who puts it forward. It is a responsibility of the whole
senior management team, particularly the Head, to explain the

situation to the staff. An awareness raising session led by the Head where the issues are clearly put to the whole staff could be a starting point for dealing with the problem of hostility to the concept. Once they have come at least to realise that it is a necessary evil, you can begin to make progress.

The argument about the school's need simply to present itself more positively to the public may in fact attract considerable support. Promoting a positive image in the community – of education in general and your school in particular – is an important part of a school's task, and one that has largely been neglected in the past. The value of improving liaison eg with the school's feeder schools, will be obvious to a lot of staff.

Although you will not convince everyone about marketing, you can reduce the initial opposition and in time it will become, if not totally acceptable, at least a more familiar part of managing a school. Always remember that the line between what is necessary and legitimate and what is educationally unacceptable is a delicate one. If you always stay firmly on the right side of that line, most people will be reassured.

2   Set up a marketing team

You will not be able to deal with all the aspects of marketing the school yourself as it will not be your only senior management responsibility and it is an extremely time-consuming job, so you will need to set up a marketing team and act as its co-ordinator. The team will probably include some governors and parents as well as staff as you will want to draw upon different talents.

3   Analyse strengths and weaknesses

One of the first questions a commercial marketing expert will ask you is 'What are your selling points? What are your school's particular strengths?' Are you a community school? Are you achieving consistently high examination results? Do you have marvellous sports facilities? Are you outstanding for musical excellence? What is it that could attract parents and pupils to choose your school?' S/he will also want to know where the weak spots are that will need glossing over or improvement. The team will have to decide how to do this analysis as staff perceptions of the school's strengths may be different from those held by parents, pupils or members of the local community.

4 Decide targets

You will need to decide what areas to target and what the time-table will be. This means that you will have to construct a development plan possibly for the next three years. An example of a marketing development plan can be found at the end of this section.

5 Allocate responsibilities

The team will need to decide how to allocate responsibilities. It is important that no individual tries to do too much and that all the members make a significant contribution. Setting, for example, six targets and making each member of the team responsible for one target area could be an effective method of deciding who does what, or they could look at different aspects of a target. If members of the team have been selected because they have particular strengths do make use of their talents, eg a member of the English Department with good communication skills could look at the language used in the school's current prospectus, while a parent who works in advertising could look at the overall presentation of the brochure.

6 Provide training if necessary

Some initial training could be useful for the members of the team. If you have a parent or a governor who is in advertising or marketing you may be able to persuade him/her to run a session for the team to help them get started and to spark off ideas. Buying this in could be expensive, and not tailored to the needs of your school, so look very carefully indeed at the commercial leaflets arriving almost daily at present offering help in marketing the school – these are simply cashing in on the schools' lack of confidence and skills. Organisations such as The Industrial Society do run good short courses on marketing and, although you would have to find the money to pay for it, it could pay dividends to send a creative member of the team on one of these courses. Where only one person can go and the course is expensive, you will want value for money, so it is important to select the member of the team who will be able to bring back most from the training for the team to use.

Case Study 14.1   *For reflection*
BESTWICK PARK HIGH SCHOOL
MARKETING MANAGEMENT PLAN

Present position
Brochures and printed documents are mostly now on the office
word processor, but although the contents are amended to include
current information, there has been no revision of either the
prospective pupils' or the Sixth Form brochures for at least four
years.

Liaison with our feeder schools is strong in some cases. No-one
hitherto has co-ordinated it and it has very much depended upon
the personalities.

Some well developed links with industry exist, but again there
has been no co-ordination of this area and the approach has been
piecemeal and intermittant, dependent upon individuals.

We have no nominated press officer. Individual teachers have
been contacting the local papers when the need arose.

A marketing management committee has now been established
to co-ordinate all the school's promotional activities.

Aims
1   To maintain pupil numbers.
2   To increase intake into the sixth form.
3   To promote a more positive image of the school to parents, the
    community and industry.
4   To obtain appropriate sponsorship for curriculum projects.

Initial tasks
1   Identify a number of key areas.
2   Generate strategies.
3   Agree approaches.
4   Allocate responsibilities for each area.
5   Decide timetable for programme.
6   Work out budget and training needs.
This was done at our first meeting held on 15th October.

Overall strategy
It was agreed that a number of key areas would be targeted –
brochures, liaison with feeder schools, links with industry and the

coverage we receive in the local press. It was decided to adopt a bit-by-bit approach to these areas, rather than putting all of our resources intensively into one area.

Timetable
Year 1
1 Begin work on prospective parents' brochure – rewrite it to make it more user friendly, look for sponsorship.
2 Plan a programme of ongoing links with feeder schools and test some elements of it.
3 Analyse all press cuttings for the previous school year and work out where more publicity is needed. Start a school Scrap Book. Nominate a school Press Officer who should start making contacts with the three local papers.
4 Analyse nature of present contacts with industry. Appoint a industry links co-ordinator work this into the school TVEI programme and explore possibilities – planning period.

Year 2
1 Revise the Sixth Form Brochure.
2 Feeder school liaison programme runs through for the first time.
3 Industry links – curriculum initiative developed and begins to be implemented.
4 Sponsorship targeted for specific projects eg a 'posh' school magazine.
5 Publicity programme begins to operate.

Year 3
1 Evaluate and revise where necessary all schemes which have now run for one year.
2 Continue brochure revision programme – third year choices booklet.
3 Links with industry in place – hopefully sponsored.
4 Plan targets for the next phase of development.

Costs
1 Printing costs for brochures
2 Costs of announcements and other necessary publicity eg advertising costs
3 Staff time

4　Training needs eg marketing courses
5　Cost of ancillary support
6　Consultancy?

7　Dealing with the press

It is no longer unusual for a school to have a member of staff who acts as press officer. This member of staff is the only person, apart from the Head, who speaks to the press. S/he deals with all inquiries from the papers and writes any press releases that the school issues to the papers. The value to a school of having a press officer is that: only one version of events goes out, the press officer can build up personal links with the reporters on the local papers, and the school could benefit from featuring regularly in the local press. This could increase pupil recruitment and create an image of an active and successful establishment.

The press officer has to see that the school does feature regularly and that the publicity is positive. He or she is unlikely to be a senior member of staff (often a grade A allowance is given for a responsibility of this nature) but s/he is likely to be a member of your marketing team and you would have to monitor his/her performance.

There is usually more than one local paper in an area and several schools. You cannot expect to be featured to the exclusion of other local schools, nor can you provide exclusive information for just one of the papers as this will arouse hostility – so will telling all the papers your news is exclusive to them when it isn't. If you regularly win your sporting fixtures you are unlikely to get much publicity for it however disappointing this is for your pupils and their parents. There is, however, a lot of interest in education and many local papers have realised this, so the opportunity is there for some good publicity for your school. Newspapers are interested in what is unusual or happening for the first time, so your press officer needs to look for a new angle on things, though make sure that it is one that puts the school in a good light. Feeding the papers with plenty of material is important because only some of it will appear. The press officer will need to know by which day in the week information has to reach the paper if it is to appear in that week's edition. Reporters usually have time to spare the day after publication and this could be a good day to contact the paper. Monitor how regularly and how favourably the school is featured so that if you are feeling slighted or badly treated you can give evidence. If for example your examination results were not featured while your rival's were on the front page – ask the education reporter into school and find out what went wrong. If your office forgot to send in the results it is not the paper's fault if they do not publish them.

Case Study 14.2   *Exemplar*
**BESTWICK PARK HIGH SCHOOL PRESS
RELEASE**

85 members of the senior and junior choirs of Bestwick Park High
School took part in the Besthampton Music and Drama Festival on
Wednesday 17th October. The junior choir received a distinction and
were placed joint first in their section. The senior choir won the
Besthampton Choirs' Cup and will perform in the prize winners'
concert on Saturday 27th October. The able accompanist for both
choirs was Janet Randolph, a member of the lower Sixth Form. The
choirs were conducted by the school's Head of Music, Peter Price,
who is also the conductor for the Besthampton Choral Society.

Marketing strategies

1   Review and improve written communications

Brochures
Schools usually have at least three main brochures – a prospectus, information about choice of courses at 14+ and a brochure about the school's sixth form. Their purpose is to attract pupils to join the school and to provide information about the courses, opportunities and facilities available. Many schools now have very attractive brochures and they have come to form an important element in promoting the school's image, so a good starting point for your marketing team could be to review how well the school's brochures are doing their job. It makes a good exercise for the marketing team, but it is also helpful if you can find a critical friend who is not involved with the school to go through the same exercise for you.

A brochure checklist:
- Is it easily understandable, ie is the language user friendly/full of jargon/difficult to follow?
- Is the print large enough or is it difficult to read?
- Is it clear who the brochure is aimed at – parents/pupils/both?
- What is the layout like? Is the print too much of a mass, so that the brochure is hard to read?
- Are there plenty of clear headings?
- Have pictures been used? Are they clear and do they confirm the written statements?
- Can you find out all that you need to know from reading it? eg Is it clear where the school is located, how a pupil is admitted, what subjects are offered?
- Is there too much detail so that people will be put off reading the brochure?
- Would it improve the brochure to include an index or contents page?
- Is there a map?
- Have all the legal requirements been included?
- Is the information up-to-date and accurate? How recently has the data in the brochure been checked?
- What kind of overall impression of the school do you get by reading this brochure?

If any of your brochures do badly in this test, you probably need to revise them. The team will need to decide whether a completely new approach is needed or whether some cosmetic revamping will suffice. This may depend upon your budget as printing is extremely expensive. As a senior manager faced with mounting requests from staff for books and equipment, you will find it difficult to justify financing a brochure out of capitation and you will probably not be able to afford to do so, yet if you cannot attract more pupils your income will fall, so either way you are in a dilemma. It is largely because of the heavy expense involved in producing glossy brochures that schools are increasingly seeking help from parents who have connections with the printing industry or they try to get at least part of the cost covered by industrial sponsorship.

If you fail to get sponsorship and haven't much to spend, here are some hints:

1   Pictures, particularly colour, are the most expensive item – use them sparingly if the school is meeting the bill out of its own budget.
2   Remember that it is the cover that makes the first impression and try to make it attractive.
3   Improving the language to make it clear is not an expensive item.
4   You can do a lot with the layout even without the use of pictures.
5   Try not to include in the brochure information that easily dates, then you can do a longer print run. Dates of terms, staff lists etc can go on separate sheets in the backflap.
6   Prospective parents find a map and the school's address and telephone number helpful – the back cover can be a good place to put them.

Producing a 'flier'
A flier is a leaflet about the school. It is much shorter and cheaper to produce than a brochure or prospectus. It conveys a 'snapshot' of the school using a few ideas and some pictures and its advantage is that it is easy both to distribute and to read. If you want to interest people in the school by having information in the local library, estate agents etc you are much more likely to use a flier than your full prospectus. Similarly you could use it for door-to-door delivery. The basic principles for producing a leaflet about the school are the same as for designing a brochure except that you need to be much more concise.

Newsletters
A newsletter is a good way of providing parents with information about the school on a regular basis. It is usually issued on a termly or half-termly basis. Sending home a newsletter indicates to parents that you expect them to be interested in the school and a full newsletter indicates a high level of activity. It can serve a number of different purposes:

- to give reminders of forthcoming events eg the school play or sports day

- to give progress reports eg on building work or fundraising
- to include appeals eg for help for scenery for the play or a parent to accompany a trip which needs a high ratio of staff to pupils
- to mould opinion eg about a new and perhaps controversial course
- to list achievements – academic, sporting, extra curricular etc

If you already have a newsletter the marketing team could consider how well it is fulfilling its function. It might benefit from being less formal and wordy, or it might, like the school's brochures, need to be presented in a more attractive manner. Some articles by pupils might encourage more of the school to read it.

Other written communications
The school frequently has to communicate with parents eg about functions, expeditions, notification of parents' meetings, dates of terms. If you are in charge of communications try to ensure that these letters and notifications of events are:

- well presented – make sure that the office is using a good word processor – the time when scrappy, illegible letters were acceptable is long past;
- accurate – getting the day or the date wrong creates an impression of incompetence;
- clear – parents and pupils need to be able to understand what the message is.

2 Improve liaison

Feeder schools
Improving links with your feeder schools could benefit you in several ways, eg:

- providing a opportunity to recruit potential pupils either directly or indirectly;
- helping pupils and staff learn more about how your school operates;
- increasing goodwill;
- creating curriculum links which help ease progression.

The number of feeder schools that send you pupils will affect the nature and strength of the links that you can develop. If you only have two or three feeder schools, you can direct all your efforts towards forming a relationship with those schools. If you have forty or fifty feeder schools, you cannot form a close relationship with them all and will have to take a different approach eg inviting a particular curriculum area such as English or Science to a teachers' meeting. Some ways of liaising with feeder schools include:

1   First-form pupils write letters back to their primary school (PSE task). This is usually much appreciated by the primary schools who like news of their former pupils.
2   Staff visit all prospective pupils in summer term before they start secondary school. This needs a small carefully-chosen team, who will be good ambassadors for you and who should be well briefed so that they can answer questions and re-assure pupils about any worries or concerns.
3   Hold an induction day for new intake during the latter part of the term before they start, so that they can experience a day in their new school. The induction should give a taste of lessons and school procedures eg lunch arrangements. The staff visits should be before the pupil induction.
4   Staff visits in the Autumn Term as a follow up to the prospective parents' meeting may be possible. This gives an opportunity to answer questions on a less formal basis than in a meeting with several hundred people. These visits can be very effective and are appreciated by the pupils, but may not be viable for your school either because they are too time consuming or because there is so much competition that the primary heads feel that this represents touting for pupils and decide not to allow any visits of this kind.
5   Invite top form junior pupils to suitable functions eg the dress rehearsal or a special preview of the school play or to a concert given by the first form.
6   Expand curriculum links. Improved curriculum links be-tween the primary and secondary sectors are an important component of the national curriculum and one whose value most teachers accept. If you only have a small number of local feeder schools it is possible to develop close classroom links including some exchange of teaching eg between the top

junior form in the primary school and the first year in the secondary school. Subject meetings for the core subjects, held on a termly basis, eg English in the Autumn term, Mathematics in the Spring Term and Science in the Summer term helps the teachers to get to know each other and to exchange ideas.

7 Invite primary teachers to visit. As well as curriculum meetings you could invite teachers to spend a day or half day in the school on an individual basis. You cannot do this too often but about once a month should not be too difficult. Primary staff may appreciate this facility being available.

8 Invite the Heads of primary schools either on a group or an individual basis so that you know the head of the school when you have to ring up to arrange about a visit. Your Head will probably have to host this activity.

9 Pupil projects that involve secondary school pupils working with primary pupils are always popular and rewarding.

10 Send news of the leavers' destinations and achievements back to their primary schools – once a year should be sufficient. Similarly send copies of the school newsletter and, if you have time, highlight items which may be of interest to them.

It would not be viable to try to implement all the elements of this programme at the same time, but if improving links with feeder schools is part of your development plan, you can set targets over a period of time so that you can work towards building better links. The person to take responsibility for liaison with feeder schools will probably be the First Year Head, though sometimes this is seen as a responsibility of the Pastoral Deputy. Whoever holds the responsibility, this member of staff is clearly an essential member of your marketing committee and, as in the case of the press officer, your role will be that of co-ordinating and monitoring the development work.

The community
Developing links with the local community can be extremely valuable for a school, because:

● local goodwill is very important to the school;
● strong links will enhance the school's image;
● it could attract pupils;

- it helps the pupils and is an element of their Personal and Social Education programme.

Some schools are very clearly 'community schools', drawing most of their pupils from the area immediately round the school and serving the community through making the use of their classroom and other facilities available to the public. If however your school draws pupils from a wide geographical area, it is more difficult for you to define what you mean by community or to know with whom to liaise.

It is important for the school that its image in the community is positive so you will need to do more than develop a few individual links. An analysis of how the school is perceived by the local community, perhaps conducted by the Social Studies or PSE classes, would also be a valuable basis for your planning. If the perceptions are largely negative or very different from how the school perceives itself, then you need to devote time and energy to changing these perceptions. Analyse also what links already exist – find out if they are all centred in one area of the school eg the Sixth Form, or whether you are only relating to one section of the community eg old people. Then decide how to involve more sections of the school – the PSE programme could be a way in here.

There are some perennial problems, for example, sixth formers parking across local residents' drives because the school's parking facilities are inadequate, complaints about the behaviour of pupils in the shops or at bus stops – which affect the school's image in the local community but are difficult for you to prevent. When you get complaints the important thing is that the school is seen to respond quickly, to take the complaint seriously and to be making an effort to redress the situation. What you have to ensure is that the school's active participation in the community, positive reports about it in the press, etc vastly outnumber the complaints.

Some ways of liaising with the community include:

1   Decide to target a specific area eg the nearby local old people's home and link it to a particular year group.
2   Hold a Xmas party/concert for old people run by the pupils. This often makes a very good Sixth Form social training project as they have to solve all the problems attached to running

the event eg transporting the guests, providing facilities for the disabled, organising the food etc.

3   Community work in local nurseries, hospitals and day centres. This tends to centre on the Sixth Form.

4   If the school collects goods eg at Harvest Festival or Xmas have some of the parcels delivered personally by pupils. This is always popular and creates a positive image of the school.

5   Liaise with the local library, if there is one nearby, to see if you can have a display area at least once or twice a year. It is particularly effective if you can occasionally run an active event in the library eg your pupils reading their stories to nursery school children.

6   Liaise with the local museum, theatre or any local organisation that exists within easy reach of the school. There may be a curriculum project that you can develop together. Again the results could be displayed in the museum or library.

7   A PSE or Technology project that is centred on the local community can benefit both sides.

Industry
The benefits to a school of creating strong links with industry are considerable:

● curricular links help the pupils appreciate the relevance of their studies.
● both school and industry develop a better understanding of how the other operates.
● the links could lead to material benefits or sponsorship for your school.
● the links could lead to opportunities for your pupils, eg work experience, employment opportunities etc.

Large national companies have most to offer schools, understand the value of links with schools and are more prepared to give up time, but they will be approached by a large number of schools. They cannot respond to every request, so what should you do?

Some ways of creating links with industry include:

1   Construct a register of parents with useful contacts and use them where possible to form the initial links. Staff spouses can also sometimes be very helpful.

2 Use the local yellow pages to see if there are major companies with local offices and contact them.
3 Have a definite project in mind.
4 Do not expect too much from any one company. The same company cannot be expected to support all your courses.
5 Think about what you can offer industry. Links should not be totally one-sided.
6 A good curriculum development project could interest a company and attract support into the school.
7 Sometimes a firm where a pupil is doing work experience could be interested in continuing and extending its contacts with the school. This means that you need to use staff work experience visits as potential for generating links.
8 Staff placements in industry can be used for the development of curriculum materials or further links.
9 Always attribute and give credit to the company for any help or support they have given the school. It maintains goodwill and encourages further support.

Do not expect links with industry to develop or bear fruit over night. They take a long time to establish and need constant nurturing; if they depend on the goodwill or interest of a particular personnel officer, they can vanish overnight if that person leaves the firm or is transferred to another area. But if you can establish strong links with a group of companies they can be a major resource for the school, industry can help with training through their training officers and courses; they can sometimes provide facilities eg for Inset sessions; they may be able to make direct input into some courses; they can provide visits and opportunities for work experience or shadowing, which will benefit your pupils; speakers from commerce and industry could contribute to your school careers' programme, and unwanted equipment, especially from computer firms, could be a useful asset for a school.

3 Displaying the school

Any visitor to your school should find it an attractive and welcoming place. The poor state of the building might be beyond your control, but how the school and its personnel present itself is a part of your management task and could be less time consuming to improve than some of the features of the school already considered in this chapter.

A checklist for displaying the school

1   Take a good look at the entrance to the school or the lobby. Does it look inviting? Are there pictures or Art work displayed on the walls, or is there a display cabinet with examples of projects or pottery that visitors can look at while they wait for attention?
2   Is it difficult for visitors to find their way to the reception area?
3   How well labelled is the school? Are there plenty of signs or directions and if there are, how well presented are they? A 'tatty' sign makes a poor impression.
4   Does the school pass the graffiti test?
5   How difficult is it for a parent to make an appointment to see the Head or a member of staff? Are your telephone lines permanently engaged?
6   Is the secretary/receptionist brusque or rude to callers? It is crucial to the image of the school that the person answering the phone to callers is friendly and courteous and that the office is welcoming and helpful when visitors arrive.
7   How are visitors treated in the school? If they are mown down by pupils on the corridors, this does not make a good first impression!
8   Who shows a prospective parent around? Pupils, particularly Sixth formers, are often very good guides, but are they briefed first about what is required of them and why it matters? Do you check up with visitors what impression your pupils are making upon them?
9   Are there plenty of pictures and other displays around the school? Are there examples of pupils' work on the walls and photographs of events, eg sports day or the school play, displayed in appropriate places?
10 Are there examples of the school's brochures and the school magazine in the waiting area where a prospective parent can peruse them?

Be available

Open days

Open days, especially prospective parents' evenings, have become
a critical element in promoting the school.

Some guidelines for an effective open day are:

1 Have a clear programme and make sure that it is given to the
  parents.
2 Make sure that everyone, staff, pupils, caretaker etc is well
  briefed about what they are expected to do and friendly and
  courteous to all guests.
3 Make sure that you do not run out of brochures.
4 Use human signposts ie pupils to supplement arrows, maps of
  the school and other directions.
5 Have more than one route so that at the peak times there are
  no 'traffic jams'.
6 Displays need to be good – colourful, easily seen if there are
  crowds of people in the room; some active displays, involving
  pupil performance are always popular.

7　If there are likely to be parking problems, liaise with the local residents before the event.
8　Be available eg in the entrance lobby or hall, so that there are plenty of senior staff to greet the guests and answer questions.
9　Monitor the event so you know for next time what went well and should be repeated and where improvements are needed.

Videos of the school

Some schools have produced promotional videos as a part of their marketing policy.

Advantages and disadvantages of making a video
The advantage of a video is that you have a valuable visual aid available that you can use if you having to give a talk etc about your school.
There are several disadvantages:
An in-house effort can look very amateurish and be counter-productive.
It is time consuming to make.
If you use professionals, it can be extremely expensive.
It dates very quickly.
It is difficult to decide who the audience is – prospective parents, feeder schools, who ...?
Watching a video can sometimes be less effective than a good talk and can prevent interaction between the audience and the speaker.
　A good and less expensive compromise could be to use slides of the school, or even to use them as the basis of the video. If you do decide to produce a video you may find it effective to use parts of it to supplement your talk rather than showing the whole of a 20 minute programme.

A short reading list

As a senior manager you are expected to be well informed about all the recent developments in education. Here are three tests that you could apply to selecting management books:

- Is the book lively and stimulating and will it help you to think clearly about your role as a manager?
- Does the book contain ideas and material which could further the development of your own management skills and understanding?
- Does the book contain a lot of information that you will need to use? Some books of this type make few concessions to readability and you will want to key into the relevant section as required.

Here are ten books which could form the basis of your library:

General school management

The first three books are written by industrialists about education. They are all pre-ERA but have more to offer than some more recent books.

1 KB Everard and G Morris – *Effective School Management*, Harper 1985. This is a stimulating introduction to management, which has stood the test of time. More than ever after LMS, it is important for you to be able to take a holistic view, and the chapters on 'management of change' remain valuable.

2 KB Everard – *Developing Management in Schools*, Blackwell 1986. This book is based on Everard's study of the problems of school management in 20 schools and his meetings with several hundred Heads and Deputies on management training courses. It provides a useful survey of the research which compares schools with industry.

3 Charles Handy and Robert Aitkin – *Understanding Schools as Organisations*, Penguin 1986. This book is a follow up to Charles Handy's *Taken for Granted? Understanding Schools as Organisations*. Handy's aim was to investigate the differences between schools and business, and the book contains his ideas about organisational cultures.

4   Joan Dean – *Managing the Secondary School*, Croom Helm 1985. Joan Dean was Chief Inspector for Surrey and her book is a mine of information. There are no concessions to readability whatsoever, but the book is an excellent resource, limited only in that it was written before LMS.

5   D Torrington and J Weightman – *The Reality of School Management*, Blackwell 1989. The authors interviewed over 1000 teachers over a period of two years. The study indicated that too much time is spent on administration and that teachers do not value the work done by senior managers. Particularly interesting, but extremely depressing for senior managers is the section on deputy heads. Many **Deputy Heads** emerged as 'essentially personal assistants to the Headteacher' and a case study of three deputies showed them all to be under utilised. This research clearly makes the case for more effective use of the senior management team.

Management books not written specifically for education

6   J Hunt – *Managing People at Work*, McGraw Hill 1986. This is a book for managers based on behavioural science. It explores motivation, perception, groups, structures, leaders, change etc. All managers should try to read at least one theoretical book and this one is good of its kind and clearly written.

7   Sir John Harvey-Jones – *Making it Happen*, Collins 1988. The distilled wisdom of the ex-chief of ICI was a best seller, even before he became a TV personality. You may find it useful to set his ideas against Charles Handy's.

Staff development

8   Feargus O'Sullivan, Ken Jones and Ken Reid – *Staff Development in Secondary Schools*, Hodder and Stoughton 1988

9   David Oldroyd and Valerie Hall – *Trist Handbook – Managing Professional Development and Inset*, MSC 1988
Both books derive from TRIST and aim to provide a guide to staff development generated out of good practice. Either provides a valuable resource for the Inset Co-ordinator.

LMS

10   B Fidler and G Bowles – *Effective Local Management of Schools*, Longman 1989. This is a very comprehensive volume with a thorough coverage of all aspects of LMS for schools. It is a compendium with contributions from a number of authors.

CIPFA *Local Management of Schools* – CIPFA's practical guide (1988) remains a useful source of reference.

Index